OUR PSYCHIC POTENTIALS

BY D. SCOTT ROGO

ANOMALIST BOOKS
San Antonio • New York

contents

───────────────preface

Many critics have argued that contemporary psychology has been interested in only the negative aspects of the human personality. They point out that its major concern has long been the study of how our unconscious minds exert an oftentimes damaging influence over our thoughts and even over our very lives. This criticism is somewhat justified. Clinical psychology and psychiatry have mostly addressed themselves in the past to such problems as how we can overcome the inhibitive effects of the unconscious, how to handle stress, and how to lift ourselves from the depths of neurosis, psychosis, and breakdown. One might even say that clinical psychology has always been a rather morbid and disheartening affair.

All this has changed, however, during the past three decades. Ever since World War II, some mental-health workers have begun to realize that certain psychological techniques can be used to help people grow, explore their creative potentials, and reach out to experience new avenues of consciousness. Even its critics have realized that present-day psychology has begun to radically change its attitude toward the human psyche. This whole new approach to the mind gave rise to the development of humanistic psychology—the psychology of human growth—in the 1950s, and a few bold psychologists even went on to develop transpersonal psychology in the 1960s. This new form of mind–science taught that each of us has the potential to "reach out" and contact deep spiritual and mystical states of consciousness. Just as Buddhism has taught for countless centuries, transpersonal psychologists also realize that there exists a spark of divinity within Man, a spark just waiting to be released. The upshot of this new way psychology has begun to look at Man and his mind has had a significant effect on our contemporary culture and in turn has led to what is called the "human potentials movement." The major theme of this movement, which sprang out of the psychedelic revolution of the 1960s, is that all of us harbor hidden creative energies deep within our minds and that each of us should try to tap and give expression to these forces. Far from being simply a mental-health movement, psychology today has become a growth-oriented field.

It is not by chance that parapsychology has made its greatest strides over the last few decades. More and more laymen, psychologists, and scientists have realized that the inner mind is as fascinating an area of study as are the farthest reaches of space or the mysterious depths of the ocean. The development of parapsychology has been a direct outgrowth of the human potentials movement as more and more people have begun to experiment with personal psychic development. This has resulted in a shifting approach to the ESP phenomenon among parapsychologists themselves. Until the 1930s most parapsychologists believed that only a few gifted individuals possessed psychic abilities. However, many contemporary parapsychologists have uncovered irrefutable evidence that psychic abilities—including everything from telepathic powers, precognitive abilities, and even mind over matter—are not "gifts" in any sense of the word. They are *potentials*. And as potentials, they are something we all inherently possess and can conceivably develop. The only problem is that few of us seem able to tap or use these abilities to any reliable degree.

This very problem serves as the central theme for this book. If we all possess psychic abilities, how can we learn to control them, use them, and develop them to their furthest extent? Many clues and techniques have been uncovered, some of which date back hundreds of years. Others have only recently been developed. In this volume, I will show the reader in a step-by-step fashion how to use certain strategies for making contact with the psychic potential as well as examine the evidence that these techniques may work for at least some people.

I personally believe that parapsychology today has proved that ESP can be enhanced, developed, or at least tapped. I feel that the research supporting this discovery is impressive. The subject of psychic development, though, is a complex and tricky one, and in this book I hope to explore many of these complexities.

For convenience, this volume will be divided into several sections. The first will be devoted to the evidence that we all are capable of tapping our psychic potentials. Reports from persons who have actually developed psychic ability as well as laboratory research will be presented showing that ESP is directly related to several altered states of consciousness. Next I will explore specific "systems" of psychic development showing the many techniques that can be used to make contact with the sixth sense and how the reader can adapt this material into a program of self-testing. These comments are designed to show how a formal self-training course in ESP can be formulated from the research that has come out of parapsychology laboratories across the country.

I cannot stress enough, however, that this book is not merely a "how to" book on psychic development. It is equally devoted to the *evidence* that we all possess psychic ability, and it will explore the scientific evidence gathered about how the ability can be enhanced or at least used. Each chapter will indeed show you *how* you can use this material personally. But just as important is the fact that this book is the only one of its kind based on sophisticated laboratory documentation and not on a congeries of speculation and psychic "mythology."

The author would like to thank the following authors and publishers for the use of copyrighted material:

The quotations from Upton Sinclair, *Mental Radio*, New York, Collier Books (reprint) 1971 are reprinted through the courtesy of Charles C. Thomas, Publisher, Springfield, Illinois.

Material from Louisa E. Rhine, *ESP in Life and Lab*, © 1967 by Louisa E. Rhine is reprinted with permission from Macmillan Publishing Co., Inc.

The excerpts from *Dream Telepathy* by Montague Ullman, Stanley Krippner and Alan Vaughan—© 1973 by Montague Ullman, Stanley Krippner, and Alan Vaughan—are used by permission of Macmillan Publishing Co., Inc. and the authors.

Extracts from "Scientific, Ethical, and Clinical Problems in the Training of PSI Ability" by Rex Stanford, are used by permission of the author.

Use of transcripts of PSI-conducive tapes in Dr. William Braud, "Clairvoyant Tests Following Exposure to a PSI-Conducive Tape Recording" is by permission of Dr. William Braud.

Material from Mr. Leonard George, *Training Manual for ESP Testing and Visualization Strategies* is by permission of Mr. Leonard George.

Portions of Chapter Three originally appeared in the September/October issue of *Psychic* Magazine, © *New Realities* Magazine (680 Beach Street, San Francisco, California 94109), and are used with permission.

Portions of Chapter Four have been adapted from "Learning to Use Your ESP," an article that originally appeared in the December 1983 issue of *FATE* Magazine (500 Hyacinth Place, Highland Park, Illinois 60035) and are reprinted by special permission of *FATE* Magazine.

Some of the judging procedures for free response material that appear in Appendix I are adapted from the *Journal* of the American Society for Psychical Research, April 1974, and are reprinted by permission of Dr. Rex Stanford and the American Society for Psychical Research.

_____introduction: learning to be psychic

The date was January 23, 1969. Joicey Acker Hurth had been a bride for only three months and was living with her husband's parents in the city of Cedarburg, Wisconsin. She was still glowing from this new development in her life, but her mood changed suddenly and overnight. That morning she woke with a feeling of deep sadness gnawing inside of her. There was no logical or apparent reason for her sudden descent into depression; she felt only an overriding sense that something was wrong at her home back in South Carolina. "I did not want to disturb my husband," she later reminisced about that dreadful morning, "so for a long while I stared wide-eyed at the ceiling of the bedroom, which was barely visible in a dim, shadowy light. I remember the terrible ache in my heart." Her husband woke up when she started to cry. She still had no idea why she felt so miserable, but at the breakfast table that morning she suddenly felt certain that something was wrong with her father ... even though, to the best of her knowledge, he was in perfect health.

Moments later the phone rang. Her aunt and her mother came on the line respectively, calling to tell Joicey that her father was in a coma. He had suffered an adverse reaction to some medication, which had disrupted the functioning of his kidneys. Within a few days he was dead.

In the spring of 1979 David Booth was an assistant manager of a car rental agency in Cincinnati, Ohio. Between May 16 and May 25 he experienced a series of vivid and horrifying dreams. Each time he would find himself looking over a field at a building resembling a schoolhouse. A plane would be flying in from the northeast, and Mr. Booth invariably found his attention riveted on the aircraft. The plane seemed to be having engine trouble—it didn't seem to be making the right sort of sound. Then the craft would invariably "roll over on its back and go straight down into the ground." As he later told a researcher at the Institute for Parapsychology in Durham, North Carolina, "When the plane hit the ground it exploded in a huge explosion. I can't think of any words to describe the explosion except that it was awesome." So shockingly vivid was this recurrent dream that Mr. Booth could even identify the plane as an American Airlines three-engine jet.

Mr. Booth relived this nightmare ten times between May 16 and May 25. He even called American Airlines and the Cincinnati Aviation Administration to report his fear that his dreams were foretelling a major air disaster. A representative from the FAA was so impressed by the story that he wrote out a description of the dream and placed it in the official files.

Yet no one at the FAA or at American Airlines could have known at the time just how prophetic Booth's dreams would turn out to be. On May 25, 1979—the day the dream stopped recurring—an American Airlines jet crashed while trying to land at Chicago's massive O'Hare Airport. It was one of the worst tragedies in modern aeronautical history. An engine literally fell off the plane's left wing, hurling the craft to earth where it exploded into a fountain of flames. Bystanders who witnessed the freak accident also reported that the plane had made odd noises before crashing, as though all of its engines had suddenly ceased operating or lost power.

Several years ago Dr. G. Dupré, an eminent French physician, placed on record a remarkable "vision" depicting an accident that was simultaneously occurring some miles away. "I had just been visiting a patient and was coming downstairs," he later recounted, "when suddenly I had the impression that my little girl of four years old had fallen down the stone stairs of my house and hurt herself. Then gradually after the first impression, as though a curtain which hid the sight from me were slowly

2

drawn back, I saw my child lying in front of the stairs, with her chin bleeding, but I had no impression of hearing her cries. The vision was blotted out suddenly, but the memory of it remained with me. I took note of the hour—10:30 A.M.—and continued my professional rounds."

When the good doctor returned home, he learned that an accident had not only occurred just as he had seen it but at the very time he had recorded. Luckily, the little girl was not seriously hurt.

All three of the people whose stories have just been recounted—Mrs. Hurth in Wisconsin, Mr. Booth in Cincinnati, and Dr. Dupré in France— shared two things in common. They all experienced brief encounters with the unseen during which they momentarily tapped into their inner psychic potentials. But none of these three astonished witnesses considered him- or herself "psychic" in the literal sense of the word. Mrs. Hurth has reported several other inexplicable "intuitions" over the years, but has never made any serious effort to develop her powers. Mr. Booth never had a recurrence of his experience, never again dreamt of any major disaster. Dr. Dupré was so stunned by his experience that he wrote an account of it to a French magazine, hoping that someone might explain what had happened to him. None of these three individuals was apparently aware that *thousands* of similar reports of ESP in everyday life have been collected by parapsychologists. Well over 10,000 reports are currently housed in overloaded file cabinets at the Institute for Parapsychology (the old Duke University Parapsychology Laboratory) in Durham alone. And the significance of these reports is overwhelmingly clear: you don't have to be "psychic" in order to experience a flash of telepathy, a precognitive dream, or a clairvoyant vision.

All of us possess a *potential* for tapping into these psychic senses. While it is only rarely that we consciously recognize when we are receiving a psychic message, the potential for deliberately inducing such experiences probably lies deep within our minds like gold ore waiting to be mined. The incidents that have been summarized in the preceding paragraphs also illustrate the wide variety of forms that psychic experiences can take. Our psychic talents are capable of manifesting themselves through a variety of routes—dreams, hunches, coincidences, visions, hallucinations, and several other mental phenomena.

Can just anyone develop psychic abilities or learn how better to control the powers we may already have? This is a question upon which, until recently, not many parapsychologists would have agreed. It is the issue with which this book is primarily concerned.

In the 19th century some of the first psychical researchers believed that, for some unknown reason, a few people were simply born with ESP powers while most others were not. Thus they spent most of their time searching out gifted psychics, never for a moment considering that the ability might be widespread among the public at large. On the other hand, a few continental European parapsychologists thought that perhaps ESP was a genetically inherited trait, just like hair color or any other physical characteristic. These researchers attempted to trace the family histories of their favorite psychics, and indeed most of these gifted individuals obliged by pointing to some distant relative who allegedly possessed similar abilities.

It was not until the 1930s that several contemporary parapsychologists here in the United States began to accumulate evidence that we *all* possess at least some ESP ability. Although it appeared that only a handful of people were capable of consistently using or controlling the ability, the researchers discovered that some vestigial ability was apparently locked deep within all of us.

The late Dr. J. B. Rhine, who is generally considered to be the father of modern parapsychology, was the first investigator to realize just how widespread ESP abilities are among the general public. Based on his own pioneering work in the 1930s at Duke University, Rhine was able to demonstrate that *one out of every five* people he tested seemed to demonstrate at least a modicum of ESP talent. He made this startling announcement in 1937, in his masterful book *New Frontiers of the Mind.* Rhine's ESP subjects had not been screened nor selected in any way before being tested, either. In fact, they were mostly Duke students who had stumbled into his laboratory, usually out of idle curiosity.

But that was not the end of his findings by any means. By studying ESP in the laboratory and examining the accounts of people who had had flashes of ESP during the course of their everyday lives, Rhine and his associates also came to realize that ESP is an *unconscious* process. The Duke team learned that when you or I have a conscious ESP experience—such as a precognitive dream, or a telepathic flash—we are witnessing the end result of what is essentially a two-stage process. It looks as though the unconscious mind first receives the message or information, which must then literally fight its way through the nervous system and into our conscious minds.

And that's where the problem arises. Too often the ESP messages become trapped in the central nervous system and are never able to give themselves expression. That's why vivid and conscious ESP experiences are apparently so rare ... and so striking when they do ultimately occur. The three dramatic cases that opened this chapter all apparently had the psychological "push" to get through the nervous system and later enter the witnesses' minds and brains.

This principle is well exemplified by a common phenomenon known as telesomatic ESP, in which extrasensory signals bypass the conscious mind completely and are registered directly by the body. This phenomenon is critical to our understanding the nature of the ESP process.

The psychologists of the future may look upon the 1960s as the era that emancipated the mind. The psychedelic revolution, the Westernization of Zen and Yoga, the rapid emergence of the self-actualization movement—all of these trends have drastically revised the view that the mind is merely a troubled repository of repressed memories continually seeking to influence our behavior and disrupt our lives. But future historians will probably look back on the 1970s as the era in which the *body* was emancipated. Now, more than ever, psychologists are beginning to view the body not merely as a machine, but as a source of emotion, a determinate of mood, and a vehicle of expression.

The body seems to have its own language. It is continually trying to impart messages to us ... and if you listen closely enough, you'll be surprised how often the body seems to respond to extrasensory influences.

I had just such an experience myself on a winter's day in 1967, although I didn't realize what was happening to me at the time. I was attending college in Cincinnati, Ohio. Each day during those frigid months I had to walk from my dorm to the music department, which was located on the other side of the campus. When the weather was foul it could be an unpleasant walk, being about a half-mile each way. One afternoon I was walking back to the dorm, tightly bundled in an overcoat and gloves, when I suddenly felt a jabbing pain stab through my chest. The sensation caught me totally off guard. I literally reeled, and ended up leaning against a nearby building completely stunned. Then it happened again. Another jabbing pain went right through my chest and I was struck with the horrible idea that perhaps I was having a heart attack. Luckily I wasn't, and I recuperated quickly as I continued my walk back to good old Scioto Hall.

I didn't think much about my experience during the rest of the day. But two days later I received a letter from home telling me that my maternal grandfather had recently suffered a heart attack in New York. I didn't really make a connection between my grandfather's coronary and my own experience at the time. Months later, though, I realized that my experience must have occurred about the time of his attack.

ESP or coincidence? Either theory can account for my experience, but I prefer to opt for the former explanation. The close correlation between the time of my grandfather's attack and my own jabbing chest pains—the only ones I have ever had in my life—lead me to believe that I actually received an ESP impression that winter's day which, for some reason, affected my *body* rather than my mind.

Today, many parapsychologists are beginning to take a renewed interest in the possibility that the human body may be a natural ESP receiver. One of the first parapsychologists to seriously study this peculiar form of ESP was Dr. Berthold Schwarz, a New Jersey psychiatrist who has been cataloging cases of "telesomatic ESP" (as he calls the phenomenon) since the early 1960s. Schwarz has not only been collecting first-hand accounts of these incidents, but has actually attempted to alert the medical community to their importance. In 1967 he published a number of these cases in the *Journal* of the Medical Society of New Jersey, and published a follow-up study six years later in the *Medical Times.*

While my chest pains signified no real problem, somatized ESP impressions are not always so harmless. On occasion the body can react quite physically to these messages and create or catalyze genuine physiological disturbances. Dr. Schwarz cites one bizarre case concerning an Army wife who had to be hospitalized when a problem arose in her pregnancy. At the time of the hospitalization, her mother (who lived hundreds of miles away) simultaneously developed uterine bleeding. The bleeding was unexpected since the woman had gone through menopause several years before. But this wasn't the woman's first bout with unexpected bleeding. The very same thing happened six months before, at the time when another of her daughters had gone into labor.

This sort of somatic transference often occurs between relatives or close friends. In other words, they most often occur as a result of relationships which seem particularly prone to nurture shared ESP experiences. In this respect, telesomatic ESP cases seem to most commonly manifest between parents and their children, siblings, and especially twins.

This fact is aptly illustrated by a report recently published in *Psi Communicación*, a Spanish parapsychology periodical, in which Dr. D. F. Gavilon Fontanet reported on a phenomenal case of shared ESP between a pair of teenaged twins. Public attention was first drawn to the girls, Marta

6

and Silvia Landa of Rio Leza, Spain, during a trip Silvia was taking to visit her grandparents who lived in a town ten miles from her home. Marta remained with her parents at the time and was busy with some household chores when she accidentally burned her hand on an iron. At the same moment, according to her grandparents' testimony, Silvia suddenly felt a searing pain in the corresponding hand and developed a reddish burn mark. The report soon received quite a bit of local notoriety, and shortly after, the parents of the girls began keeping notes on their daughters' shared ESP. They, too, were able to verify that the symptoms from a physical mishap suffered by one girl would sometimes instantaneously transfer to the other, no matter what distance separated them. For instance, on one occasion, notes the Landas, Silvia's foot caught in a safety belt while she was trying to get out of the family car. They were returning home from a trip at the time, and Marta had already entered the house and was out of her sister's sight. Yet she suddenly found her foot paralyzed.

The case of Spain's telepathic twins soon aroused so much local publicity that it invariably came to the attention of the Spanish Parapsychological Society, which immediately requested permission to test the girls. The Landas consented, and a subsequent investigation was conducted in their own home. For one series of tests, the experimenters subjected Marta to a series of physical ordeals in one room, while a second group of experimenters monitored Silvia in another part of the house. They were able to demonstrate experimentally that Silvia would flinch when a beam of light was shone into her sister's face, and that she would contract and kick her leg whenever her sister's patellar reflex was evoked.

These types of telesomatic tranferences do not occur *only* between people who are genetically related. Several instances can be found in books and journals devoted to psychic phenomena where similar responses occurred between friends and even casual acquaintances.

But just how common are cases of psychosomatic ESP? Are they a genuinely frequent type of ESP, or are they only anomalies which sometimes grow out of the telepathic process?

It is difficult to give a precise answer to these questions, since many people who experience strange physical reactions may never realize their true psychic nature. A person who has a vivid precognitive dream or telepathic vision, for example, will probably be more likely to realize the meaning of his experience than a person who merely experiences an inexplicable ESP-mediated cramp or pain. He will also be much more prone to report it to a parapsychologist. Few people pay all that much attention to their bodies; so many of these incidents probably go unnoticed. However, we do have at least some rough statistics available on the frequency of psychosomatic ESP reactions. These data were assembled by the wife of J. B. Rhine, the late Dr. Louisa Rhine, who helped found the Parapsychology Laboratory at Duke University where they pioneered the laboratory study of ESP.

Back in the 1950s, Mrs. Rhine began collecting and cataloging reports sent to the laboratory by people who had had ESP experiences in their daily lives. Today these cases number in the thousands, and Mrs. Rhine issued an initial report on 825 of these cases of "spontaneous" ESP in 1956. She found that 123 of them dealt with telesomatic reactions. (The others dealt with ESP "visions," auditory experiences, and the like.)

Some further statistics on this subject have been offered by Dr. Ian Stevenson, a psychiatrist who heads a division of parapsychology studies at the University of Virginia. In a report on 160 telepathic "impression" cases (ESP occurrences in which the witness has only an "intuitive feeling" about a distant person without a dream or vision about him), Stevenson notes that in fourteen cases the percipients developed "definite physical symptoms during the ... experience." Some of these cases are spectacular and range from persons having simple physical sensations as the result of telepathic impressions to one person who even developed jaundice!

Stevenson has also been able to substantiate the strange fact that telesomatic reactions can become debilitating to the witness. Sometimes, according to the Virginia psychiatrist, the percipient of an ESP message will feel so ill that he or she will be totally incapacitated by it.

The evidence for the existance of telesomatic ESP does not, however, rest solely on anecdotal evidence. Experimental parapsychologists have been wondering ever since the 1960s if the body might not be an even more reliable ESP detector than the mind itself. They have also begun to wonder if the body might *habitually* register those ESP impressions which have either bypassed or failed to register on the conscious mind.

There is evidence that it does.

This discovery was first made quite accidentally in the 1950s by a Czech neurophysiologist, S. Figar. Figar was not primarily interested in parapsychology at the time, and made his discovery while carrying out conventional research on human blood volume. The scientist was using a plethysmograph, an apparatus that can be attached to any extremity of the

8

body, to monitor his subject's blood volume. He knew, of course, that whenever a person is asked to carry out a mental task (such as solving an arithmetic problem) the plethysmograph will record a vasoconstriction as blood flows toward the brain and away from other parts of the body. (This constriction shows up as a "dip" on a read-out graph. Since they are produced automatically by the body, we never consciously know when they are occurring.) While studying these vasoconstrictions Figar began noticing something quite unusual. He found that some of his subjects began producing vasoconstrictions when he merely *thought* about asking them to calculate answers to mathematical problems. He wondered if somehow his process of thinking was registering directly on the nervous systems of his subjects.

After making these observations, Figar went on to design a simple sort of ESP test in order to verify his discovery. He placed two subjects on either side of a curtain and attached both of them to delicate recording equipment. One subject, the "sender" or "agent," was asked to calculate arithmetic problems while the other subject, the "receiver" or "percipient," merely rested comfortably. As he expected, Figar found that sometimes the receiver would produce vasoconstrictions (quite unconsciously) when the agent began his mental tasks.

Soon after the Czech scientist's work became known, attempts to replicate the "Figar effect" under more rigorous experimental conditions were conducted in this country by Douglas Dean, an electrical engineer by profession (Dean's first work was sponsored by the New York-based Parapsychology Foundation and he later moved to the Newark College of Engineering). After conducting several pilot studies, Dean eventually developed a standard procedure for his experiments. As usual, two subjects were used. One subject was placed in an isolated room where his blood volume was continually monitored. His job was just to lie down and, actually, do nothing at all! The agent was given a series of cards to look at sequentially. Each was printed with either the name of someone emotionally significant to himself, significant to the receiver, or a random name drawn from the phonebook. Other cards were left blank. Dean and his collaborators designed this experiment on the hypothesis that the receiver would produce vasoconstrictions whenever the agent was concentrating on names emotionally meaningful to himself.

Dean's experimental plan was successful, though his prediction was not. Time and time again he found that his subjects produced vasoconstrictions when names of their *own* friends and relatives were the targets. Dean was able to replicate this effect several times, and this alerted him to the fact that telepathic "agents" may have little active role in the ESP process. Instead, it appears that the mind scans about looking for meaningful messages and then responds to them.

Although Dean pioneered the study of psychophysiological-ESP testing, several other innovative researchers have extended his work and findings by using other indexes. One of the most ingenious experiments was conducted in the 1960s by Charles Tart, currently a professor of psychology at the Davis campus of the University of California. Each subject for the test was placed in a room where he was hooked to a plethysmograph, an electroencephalograph (EEG), and a polygraph. That way the subject's blood volume, brain waves, and galvanic skin response (the ability of the skin to conduct an electrical current) were monitored. The subject was only told to try to guess when a "subliminal stimulus" was being sent to him. Of course, there really wasn't any subliminal stimulus since the experiment was really an ESP test. And the "telepathic message" was a rather abrupt one. Tart himself acted as agent by hooking himself to a generator which randomly administered electrical shocks, hoping that his pain and misery would telepathically transfer to his subjects!

The results of the experiment were somewhat in line with what Tart had expected. His subjects failed miserably in their attempts to "guess" when their experimenter was being shocked. But their physiological recordings indicated abrupt alterations and complications when the shocks were being administered. So while the subjects were not consciously aware of receiving the ESP messages, their bodies were quite busy receiving and processing this information.

A good example of the body/mind/ESP connection is exemplified by some fascinating research conducted in the late 1970s at the (former) Brooklyn-based Maimonides Medical Center's division of parapsychology and psychophysics.* Michael Kelly, then a gifted young research assistant working towards his Ph.D. at the Union Graduate School in Ohio, studied some of these areas while completing his dissertation. For his pilot experiment, Kelly tested his subjects individually in an isolation chamber. Inside, their eyes were covered with translucent spheres, and white noise was played into their ears. This condition of partial sensory deprivation produces a relaxed state during which daydream-like images tend to arise into consciousness. The subjects were asked to do nothing but free associate about their thoughts and mental imagery for about forty minutes or

*The Maimonides Laboratory was later reorganized in Princeton, New Jersey as the Psychophysical Research Laboratories where it is currently engaged in computerized ESP and PK research.

so while their skin conductance levels, conductance responses, skin temperatures, and muscular activity were all simultaneously monitored. An agent was placed in a separate room and, at a random time, was made to watch a five-minute emotionally arousing movie. (A film of a human birth was used in the first complete pilot study.) Kelly predicted that somehow his subjects would show changes in their physiological responses at the time the agent was watching the movie.

Kelly's general prediction was right. Although his subjects did not show any gross changes in their physiological readings during the sending time, their skin conductance levels showed significant alterations. In other words, it seemed the subjects were becoming aroused at the very moment when the agent was being emotionally stimulated. As Kelly also noted, only rarely did the subjects seem to mentally realize what the agent was going through. But their bodies obviously did.

Of course, Kelly's research is only one of several such studies being conducted by parapsychologists today. Related research is being carried out by Dr. William Braud of the Mind Science Foundation in San Antonio, Texas, and, until recently, by Drs. Edward Kelly and John Artley at Duke University.

So just what does this all mean? Are there any wide-reaching implications that we can draw from the study of telesomatic ESP? Some researchers would no doubt argue that these research findings are the result of a repression mechanism in the mind and/or brain. It may be that the central nervous system routinely inhibits extrasensory information from entering consciousness in order to attend to more relative sensory tasks. If this is true, ESP messages might then seek to express themselves by way of alternative routes. Causing mild disruptions in the body might be one such avenue of expression. I prefer to take a more holistic view of the situation, however. These cases and findings indicate that the human organism *as a whole* is naturally attuned to processing ESP information. Sometimes the mind is affected and sometimes the body is disrupted, depending on the nature of the psychic stimulus and what is, at the time, an easier route. But the information itself is directly encoded into the organism almost holographically.

No matter how you wish to explain telesomatic ESP, the research I have just cited indicates that ESP is not a rare one-shot phenomenon in which a piece of information is transmitted. It seems to be a dynamic function transmitting all the time below the threshhold of waking consciousness. This simple fact holds the key for those of us who are concerned with whether or not psychic ability can be learned and developed:

Learning to be psychic does not entail sending the mind "out" someplace and bringing information back to the brain and body. ESP is not a process like radar in which we must be alert for any significant incoming signals. It is a process of going deep within the self and retrieving information that is already there.

I suggest you reread the above paragraph several times until this concept is totally understood. It is the brick from which the rest of this book will be built.

The really ironic thing is that, while this model and its implications have evolved relatively recently within academic parapsychology, gifted psychics have long known that certain strategies help them gain access to their powers. Parapsychologists today are only discovering what many psychics have known for years! To be psychic, you need only go deeply within yourself.

The researcher who first discovered that many psychics habitually use such strategies was Rhea White, who carried out her work while she was a research associate at the American Society for Psychical Research in New York in the 1960s. Her interest in this whole area of study was piqued during some conversations she had with the wife of one of the society's donors, an intelligent woman, very psychic, who used a standard formula to tap her ESP potentials consisting of muscular relaxation, the generation of mental imagery, and self-suggestion. This led Ms. White to study the autobiographical accounts of the famous psychics of the past and present. She delved into the early Duke University work where Dr. J. B. Rhine had discussed the strategies his most gifted laboratory subjects had employed; the deeply introspective and insightful writings of Craig Sinclair (the wife of the famous novelist Upton Sinclair), who was also a remarkably talented psychic; René Warcollier, one of France's greatest parapsychologists who eventually became his own best subject; and many others. Her final report on these studies, which was issued in 1964, was an eye-opener. While each of the psychics she studied had his or her own personal idiosyncrasies, White found that they all tended to use similar techniques when wishing to use their ESP powers.

The psychics tended to go about their work step-by-step; they tended to begin by physically relaxing themselves. White reported in her study that "the early reports place a great deal of emphasis on achieving a state of deep mental relaxation. Deliberate attempts [were] made to still the body and mind, and these techniques [were] in most cases incorporated into a kind of ritual." This step was apparently very important since the psychics would often spend several minutes relaxing by the use of

12

standard relaxation exercises. They then tended to engage in some sort of activity which preoccupied the conscious mind and sort of "put it out of the way," but without entering into a trance. Some psychics were inclined to focus passively on a mental image. The next step was less concrete. The psychics would give themselves a mental command, almost like an autohypnotic injunction, for ESP to surface into consciousness. This entailed waiting until the needed information indeed surfaced. The mediating vehicle for the information was usually a mental image, an intuition, or just a sudden grasp of the material needed or requested.

These techniques may seem very simple, but they are more complex than might meet the eye. It took White some sixteen pages of quotes and commentaries to set out the particulars of these strategies. I won't go into her findings in detail at this time, since I will be alluding to her study and evidence in upcoming chapters. The most important thing to remember for now is that these strategies, taken as a whole, represent a comprehensive *system* for gaining access to the psychic sense. They are not merely convenient and idiosyncratic mental tricks the psychics chanced upon.

This approach to psychic functioning was especially recommended by Craig Sinclair, who was adamant about the self-discipline and practice that goes into being psychic. She was one of the most remarkable and fascinating subjects in the history of parapsychology. Upton Sinclair conducted dozens upon dozens of tests in which she successfully reproduced drawings he and others made up and tried to send to her. (He chronicled these experiments in his book, *Mental Radio,* published in 1930.) This gave Mrs. Sinclair the opportunity to critically examine and practice her mental strategies. In her own writings commenting on these picture-drawing tests, she had the following to say about the use of mental strategies to enhance ESP:

> The details of this technique are not to be taken as trifles. The whole issue of success or failure depends on them. At least, this is so in my case. Perhaps a spontaneous sensitive, or one who has a better method, has no such difficulties. I am just an average conscious-minded person who set out deliberately to find a way to test this tremendously important question of telepathy and clairvoyance, without having to depend on a "medium" who might be fooling himself, or me. It was by this method of careful attention to a technique of details that I have found it possible to get telepathic messages and to see pictures on hidden cards ... This technique takes time, and patience, and training in the art of concentration ...

Rhea White came to the same conclusion as the result of her own project. She comments forcefully in her 1964 report that "the purpose of introducing a deliberate method is to discipline and train the conscious mind so that it will no longer inhibit the spontaneous emergence" of ESP. Ms. White admitted candidly that "perhaps we shall never be able to produce ESP at will," but added that by the use of mental training "... we can put ourselves in the proper frame of mind to receive psi [psychic] impressions." It was White's great hope that her studies would not remain solely an exercise in scholarship, but that her colleagues would use what she had uncovered to *train* their subjects to be better psychics.

It is unfortunate that, by and large, Rhea White's work fell on deaf ears. Parapychologists actively working in the field during the 1960s were primarily conducting their tests by making their subjects guess the symbols printed on standard ESP cards.* To expedite matters, the usual procedure entailed having the subjects rapid-fire their responses. It almost seemed as if researchers in those years didn't have the time to assure very good results for themselves! It wasn't until the 1970s that parapsychologists began taking a less behavioristic approach to ESP testing. The psychedelic revolution and the consciousness movement were in full swing by then, and many parapsychologists began taking a renewed interest in the subjective experiences of the people whose talents they were studying. They also became more interested in the process underlying ESP and how to make this capricious faculty more consistent and reliable. Merely chalking up more statistical proofs of ESP eventually went by the wayside. The gradual change in parapsychology from proof-oriented to process-oriented research led some researchers to wonder if ESP could in some way be tapped by the use of dreams, relaxation, the use of mental imagery, hypnosis, and a host of other strategies by which a person can be taught to enter into an active dialogue with his or her own unconscious mind. Rhea White's paper was rediscovered at this time and provided some additional hints about how such strategies might be formulated.

The results of this research have indeed indicated that ESP is not only a widespread human potential, but that certain techniques, procedures, and states of awareness are conducive to the emergence of ESP.

The remainder of the book will be drawn from this laboratory evidence. It will argue that some general procedures for psychic self-

---

* A typical ESP test of this type utilizes a pack of twenty-five cards randomly printed with either a cross, star, set of wavy lines, star, or circle. The subject guesses a run of twenty-five cards, and he or she is expected to "call" five by chance. The results of a given experiment are compiled by summing the correct guesses for a lengthy series of such runs.

enhancement have been uncovered and documented. How this research suggests routines and exercises for your own psychic development will also be outlined.

The upcoming chapters will present five specific techniques by which the reader of this book might possibly tap into his psychic potentials. Why so many? Because every individual is different. Every individual has his or her own way of thinking, conceptualizing, gaining access to his unconscious mental life, and tapping his or her inner potentials. I doubt very much if any magical or sure-fire training method exists for developing ESP that will work for everyone. Techniques that work for one person may not work for somebody else. This is why I am very critical of commercial ESP development courses as well as most books that try to teach you how to be psychic. (I will go into this topic in greater depth in Chapter 7.) It is up to each individual to find his own method by experimenting with the various strategies outlined here, either alone or in concert with the others. No one can guarantee to make you into a psychic virtuoso; you must practice and discover the way or ways that work best for you. My purpose in writing this book is to act as a guide, not a mentor.

References

Dean, E. Douglas. The plethysmograph as an indicator of ESP. *Journal* of the Society for Psychical Research, 1962, *41*, 351–3.

Dupré, G. Letter to *Annales des Sciences Psychiques,* 1905, *1*, 324–5.

Figar, S. The application of plethysmography to the objective study of so-called extrasensory perception. *Journal* of the Society for Psychical Research, 1959, *40*, 162–74.

Haight, Jo Marie. Predicting an air crash. *Fate,* May, 1983.

Kelly, Michael; Varvoglis, Mario and Keane, Patrice. Physiological response during psi and sensory presentation of an arousing stimulus. In *Research in Parapsychology-1978,* Metuchen, N.J.: Scarecrow Press, 1979.

Rhine, Louisa E. Hallucinatory psi experiences. I. An introductory survey. *Journal of Parapsychology,* 1956, *20*, 233–56.

Schwarz, Berthold. Possible telesomatic reactions. *Journal of the Medical Society of New Jersey,* 1967, *64*, 600–3.

Sinclair, Upton. *Mental Radio.* New York: Collier Books, 1971 (Reprint).

Stevenson, Ian. *Telepathic Impressions.* Charlottesville, Va.: University of Virginia Press, 1970.

White, Rhea. A comparison of old and new methods of response to targets in ESP experiments. *Journal* of the American Society for Psychical Research, 1964, *48,* 21–56.

strategy 1

the role
of dreaming

The plight of the parapsychologist today is actually quite similar to the one which Sigmund Freud grappled with about 80 years ago. He, was looking for methods which would help his patients retrieve information and memories buried deep within their unconscious minds. Freud eventually discovered that hypnosis, dreams, and free association were tools he could use to help his patients confront these unchartered areas of the human psyche. He even dubbed dreams as the "royal road" to the unconscious. Parapsychologists, too, have been finding that similar techniques can help people gain access to their inner psychic potentials. The search for ESP-conducive states of mind has become one of the most productive areas of contemporary parapsychology and has opened a whole new chapter in the controversy over whether or not ESP can be developed and learned.

In true Freudian tradition, dreaming was one of the first roads to ESP that parapsychologists were able to isolate. Everyone dreams, and dreams seem to be natural carriers of ESP messages. Just about all researchers who have studied the way in which ESP manifests in everyday life have made this discovery. While working at the Duke University Parapsychology Laboratory in the 1940s and 50s, for example, Dr. Louisa Rhine started collecting and analyzing cases of spontaneous ESP which people from all over the country who had heard of the research were sending to the lab almost daily. These included cases of telepathic "hunches," dreams of the future, inexplicable feelings of depression when someone close to the reporter had suddenly died, etc. She eventually collected some 3290 cases of which 60 percent were either cases of dream telepathy or dream precognition.

Parapsychologists working in several foreign countries were able to replicate these discoveries. A researcher in Germany made a collection of a thousand instances of spontaneous ESP during the 1950s and found that 63 percent of them constituted dream cases. Two researchers surveying the psychic experiences reported by school children in India found that over half of their caseload was linked to dreaming. Similar findings have been made in England. Dreams seem especially linked to precognition. Mrs. Rhine made a study of spontaneous precognitive experiences in 1954 and found that 75 percent of the 3000 cases then in her files occurred within the course of dreaming.

Parapsychologists today owe a great debt to Louisa Rhine, who spent years studying the nature, dynamics, and meaning of psychic dreams. One of her major discoveries was that psychic dreams could be broken down into two major categories. Since dreams are very personal experiences, they are often architectured out of a deeply personal and symbolic language each of us has developed. So while some cases of dream ESP seem to literally foresee or predict a future event, other dreams tend to present this information in a symbolized or dramatized scenario. The psychic information will invariably be there, sometimes even intact, but it will often take a bit of detective work to discover it or sort it out. Anyone who is interested in using dreams as a vehicle for psychic development should become familiar with both these types of psychic dreams.

The following two case reports will illustrate these very different ways in which ESP information can intrude into our sleeping hours.

A good example of a realistic precognitive dream is presented by Mrs. Rhine in her book *ESP in Life and Lab*. The report had been sent to the Duke University Parapsychology Laboratory by a woman living in Minnesota:

> It was five years ago; I was eighteen years old. I awoke one morning after a restless night with a very vivid dream imprinted on my mind. I often wake remembering my dreams, but this one bothered me particularly. My mother

at that time slept on a Hide-a-bed in the living room, I in a bedroom adjoining. My dream started with Mother and me standing in a certain spot in the living room, looking down at the body of one of our best friends lying dead on the Hide-a-bed. Everything was exact. I was standing a certain way, my mother the same. She sobbed five words, "She was my *best* friend." The dream ended and I woke up. I simply couldn't get this dream out of my mind, but I shrugged it off more or less because it seemed very unlikely that this friend would be dying anywhere, but particularly unlikely that it would be on *our* Hide-a-bed. She was in perfect health at that time and still is today.

Exactly one month from the day of the dream it happened, but the situation was reversed. My mother died in her sleep of a heart attack. I awoke to hear her gasping, called the doctor and this friend immediately. The doctor arrived first and pronounced my mother dead. My friend came in and we both assumed the exact positions as in my dream—and she said the very words in the same tone of voice.

Notice how this dream presents a literal preview of the precognized event. The nature and scenario of the event are not fragmented, a great deal of information is imparted about the future incident, but note too how the dreamer's mind has altered the scene in order to disguise its emotional impact. Mrs. Rhine has suggested that in this case, the dreamer's unconscious mind may have sought to obscure the truth a bit. "The dream maker preferred to dodge the fact, and the substitution was the way to do it with very little effort." she speculates.

The lesson for you to remember here is that dreams, while they often reflect psychic information, will sometimes distort it as well.

This process of distortion crops up even more artfully in symbolic or unrealistic dreams. Mrs. Rhine cites such a case she received from a sailor who served aboard ship during World War II:

I had a dream that I was back in Norfolk, that my wife, several friends, and I were in a row boat and we were pulling into the boat landing after a fishing trip. There were a number of boats tied up at this landing, and just as we were going in between two of these boats a sudden swell appeared and my wife (who was standing up in our boat) fell over the side. Her head was mashed flat. I managed to grab her arm and pull her back into the boat. I saw some people on the pier and asked if there was a doctor present, at the same time they helped to pull her body up onto the pier.

One of the men knelt down and examined her and said, "She is all right, but her tonsils will have to be removed." I awoke immediately at this point. I noticed the time by my wrist watch. Sometime later I received a letter from my wife in which she said she had had her tonsils removed. She even had the date and time she was on the operating table. I compared this time with our time in the Pacific (the time I was awakened from my dream), and at the very moment I was dreaming of her, she was on the operating table.

This dream is typical in the way it takes a simple message, and then builds an elaborate drama around it. The interrelation between the dream content and the ESP message can vary. Sometimes ESP messages will be incorporated into a totally unrelated dream scenario, while at other times it seems that the psychic information is serving as the basis for the entire dream.

The cases and statistics that I have cited above demonstrate that ESP is prone to manifest during our dreams. That's fairly obvious. But is there any evidence that dreams can actually be manipulated into carrying ESP impressions?

The answer is an unequivocal yes, and opens a fascinating chapter in the history of ESP research.

The first investigator to realize that dreaming might be experimentally used as a road to ESP was Dr. Montague Ullman, who, being a psychiatrist by training, first began studying the psychic world of dreams as a result of some bizarre experiences he encountered during the course of his private practice. He often questioned his patients about their dreams and was startled to discover that his patients would sometimes report dreams which seemed to telepathically reflect or encapsulate incidents drawn from his own life ... and often embarrassing ones! Once, for instance, Ullman decided to keep a soapdish which wasn't his, but which a workman had left at his home. Naturally he felt some conflict over this minor moral transgression. It wasn't long before one of his patients reported a dream in which this transgression played an important role. It seemed as though the patient had pried into the therapist's mind in order to discover what conflicts lurked there. A nice switch, perhaps. ESP often manifests with comic irony!

Apart from merely documenting such incidents in his clinical practice, Ullman also began to wonder if telepathic dreams could be experimentally induced in people who would not normally consider themselves to be in any way "psychic." Like so many pioneers, he decided to test out his theory on himself.

Ullman recruited a co-experimenter for these novel tests. Since he had close professional ties with the New York-based American Society for Psychical Research at that time, he interested Mrs. Laura Dale, a staff researcher, in his project. Their joint research was conducted intermittently from 1953 to 1955. Each night during the tests, Ullman and Dale placed microphones under their pillows as they were about to retire. These microphones hooked up to tape machines which would activate at a predetermined time. The message on the tape would merely be a nonsense syllable or a suggestion to dream. Thus, at the very same time of night, the two experimenters—though living twenty miles apart—would receive similar "stimuli." Ullman hoped that by synchronizing their minds, they might telepathically tune in on each other and experience similar dreams.

The results of the experiment were provocative to say the least. Not only did they sometimes have similar dreams, they often would dream *about* incidents which had occurred during the course of their partner's life.

Of course, this project was informal and the results were hard to analyze. But it had one major upshot. It motivated Ullman to develop an even more sophisticated approach to the study of dream telepathy.

The strong arm of coincidence was working in Ullman's favor as well. Although parapsychologists had long realized that dreaming *was* a royal road to ESP as Freud well knew, before the 1950s there was simply no way to experimentally monitor dreaming. It was impossible to tell when a sleeping person was dreaming. But a breakthrough was made in the early 1950s when two researchers at the University of Chicago, Dr. Nathaniel Kleitman and Dr. E. Aserinski, made a significant discovery while studying the sleep habits of infants. They noticed that the babies periodically shifted their eyes back and forth as they slumbered. They soon expanded their observations to adults when a third researcher, William Dement, joined the project. It was then that they found that, if awakened, sleeping subjects producing REMs (rapid eye movements) reported that they had been dreaming. So to study dreaming, the Chicago team began hooking their sleeping subjects to an electroencephalograph (EEG) which monitored their brain waves and eye movements. As soon as the subject was entrenched in a REM period he was awakened and asked to talk about his dreams. A new chapter in the study of dream research had opened.

These studies set the stage for Ullman's subsequent dream-ESP research. In 1962 he was able to establish a dream laboratory at the Maimonides Medical Center, in Brooklyn, where he was working as chief administrator. The facilities weren't fancy. They were hidden away in a wing of the Community Mental Health Building—in the cellar! The suite of rooms was large enough, though, to include a conference room, several offices, an isolation chamber, and an experimental room. The lab was founded and funded for the specific purpose of experimenting with ESP and dreaming and Ullman was able to recruit a rich team of talented people to join him. His first co-worker was Sol Feldstein, a doctoral student at the City College of the City University of New York. He was later joined by Dr. Stanley Krippner and, later still, by Charles Honorton, who eventually became director of the lab until it moved out of the hospital in 1979. Although the original Maimonides dream-ESP research was completed over ten years ago, it set the stage for even more successful research being conducted along roughly similar lines today, which seems to demonstrate that ESP is a potential more than a gift or talent. The following type of experiment, which was carried out at Maimonides back in the 1960s, is typical of the kind of research in which the laboratory staff was engaged for several years.

An "unselected" subject (that is, a subject who made no claim to psychic ability, or a proverbial "man off the street") would be invited to spend a night or two at the lab. He would be tucked comfortably into bed in a special room where electrodes would be attached to his scalp, etc. These led to another room where they were linked to an electroencephalograph which monitored the subject's brain waves and eye movements during the course of the night. An experimenter monitored the equipment all night long in an adjoining room. Whenever the EEG charts indicated that the subject's eyes were moving back and forth, this informed the experimenter that his subject was dreaming. An agent (or "sender") would be stationed in another lab room and would randomly select an art print from a group of similar pictures. He would then concentrate on sending the theme of the print to the sleeping subject every time he began to dream. Each time the subject was well into a dream he would be awakened abruptly by the experimenter and asked to report his imagery over an intercom. The next day, the subject would be shown several art prints and would be asked to pick out the one he thought had been sent to him telepathically as he slept the night before.

The Maimonides team had exceptionally good luck with this procedure and with several revisions and alterations of it. For instance, one night during their first experiments in the summer of 1964, the art target was Tamayo's savage painting, *Animals*. This grotesque painting depicts two vicious dogs fighting over a piece of meat, tugging and ripping it apart. The sleep subject that night—who, remember, did not claim to have any great psychic talent—was a woman teacher and a friend of Feld-

22

stein's. She incorporated the theme of the painting into her dreams in a most unusual way. She reported the following about one of her dreams during the test night:

> I was at this banquet ... and I was eating something like rib steak. And this friend of mine was there ... and people were talking about how she wasn't very good to invite for dinner because she was very conscious of other people getting more to eat than she got ... That was the most important part of the dream, that dinner ... It was probably Freudian like all my other dreams—you know, eating, and all that stuff, and a banquet. Well, there was another friend of mine, also in this dream. Somebody that I teach with, and she was eyeing everybody to make sure that everybody wasn't getting more than she was, too. And I was chewing a piece of ... rib steak. And I was sitting at the table, and other people were talking about this girl ... and they were saying that she's not very nice to invite to eat because she's greedy, or something like that.

Notice how the theme of the print was reorganized and symbolized by the subject's mind in this dream. But the ESP message was there nonetheless.

During the succeeding years, the Maimonides team was able to demonstrate that their dream subjects could pick up more than just telepathic messages. Sometimes the experimenters asked their subjects to dream about art pictures that wouldn't be selected until the day *after* the dream session. Some of these precognition tests were just as successful as the dream–telepathy experiments.

The Maimonides dream work received an added boost when they began conducting experiments with Dr. Robert Van de Castle, himself a psychologist and an authority on dreaming. The Van de Castle work is important not only because of the extremely good results the lab achieved when he served as a subject, but because Van de Castle—who is by no means a psychic—gradually *learned* how to isolate those portions of his dreams that contained telepathic elements. The Van de Castle work thus provided parapsychology with some tentative evidence that one could learn just how to identify psychic dreams and distinguish them from normal ones.

Van de Castle first collaborated with the Maimonides workers during a series of experiments which extended from January through November of 1967. He had developed a strong interest in ESP while he was a researcher at the Institute for Dream Research in Miami, Florida. It was there that he met Montague Ullman, became intrigued with the Maimonides studies, and soon made the trip to New York to act as a subject. His trip was most opportune, for the skeptical psychologist soon turned out to be an exemplary ESP subject. The target for his first test, for example, was Salvador Dali's painting, *Discovery of America by Christopher Columbus*. This large and intricate painting shows Columbus dreaming about his upcoming voyage to the Americas. The Virgin Mary is conspicuous in the picture by her appearance on a banner borne by the explorer. Young men holding banners appear in the background, accompanied by a band of Catholic acolytes dressed in white robes.

Van de Castle picked up this religious element during his first dream of the night. Upon being awakened he told the experimenter:

> Something to do with a Polish mother ... Something to do with motherhood ... I came out there into the room, and ... it seemed as if ... that had been changed into a church ... A big Mass was going on. It seemed now that it was a whole big church in there and it was just crowded with people on all sides, and it was very filled and it was like church or Mass was now going to begin ... In the church some of the people seemed to be dressed in white robes ... Some fairly youngish male figure ... There was this person and another one, and they were now talking about the girl ... in Atlantic City or Atlantic Beach ...

The next morning he gave his experimenter more information about his dream before actually being shown the target:

> It just seemed like it had been sort of a shrine or it had been something of national importance, something of historical significance. The Mass, I think I associated with the Catholic Church only because as a youngster I had been raised for a few years as a Catholic before I gave it up, so most of my associations seem to be that this was a very elaborate affair. It seems as if the people were wearing the kind of little white frocks that altar boys wear, and it seems that there was a whole row of these across the front ... It was solemn and dignified and mysterious in a way.

Successes such as these went on night after night. What is so fascinating, though, is that over the course of Van de Castle's dream experiments, the psychologist began to develop the ability to isolate exactly *where* in his dreams the ESP message was likely to appear. He learned that the ESP message often did not normally incorporate itself into the context of the dream. If he were dreaming an involved sequence of images related to a journey to the North Pole, for example, it was unlikely that "North Pole" was the theme of the target. But if he dreamed of visiting the North Pole and some anomalous and out of place image popped up, *that* was the image usually related to the ESP target. For instance, if a lion suddenly appeared in his dream about his Artic adventure, the incongruity of the image was a sure sign that it was related to the telepathically "sent" target.

So by carefully monitoring his dreams, Van de Castle was able to develop a better ability to recognize paranormal factors when they protruded themselves into his dreams. So one might say that learning of some type took place the more Van de Castle paid attention to his dreams.

Of course the success of the Maimonides dream work does not end with Van de Castle's success, nor with the achievements of other "star" subjects that came to their attention. The dream ESP project went through several refinements during the 1960s, and dozens of one-night experiments were conducted with volunteer subjects who often produced surprisingly good results. Some of the lab's most successful subjects were local college students who had no real interest in the tests except for the fact that they were paid for their services! Even these perhaps begrudging subjects many times scored spectacularly well at the tests. Long distance tests between New York and other cities in the United States fared just as well.

The Maimonides researchers also took an innovative approach to the study of precognitive dreaming. They were eager to see if they could capture the precognitive dream in the laboratory; something no one had ever done before. As I pointed out earlier, precognitive dreaming is one of the most common forms of psychic experience, so the exploration of precognition was a logical extension of the Maimonides dream experiments. But the breakthrough was rather slow in coming. Active research into the nature of precognitive dreaming had to wait until 1969. That was the year when a young psychic visited the lab from Great Britain, and his remarkable talent for dreaming the future brought him to the forefront of attention in the parapsychology community.

Malcolm Bessent was a personable young Englishman, who was still in his 20s when he first agreed to participate in the Maimonides study. During his visit to Brooklyn, he spent several nights in the dream lab attempting to dream about a specially constructed experience he would undergo the next day at the hands of his experimenters. Bessent would first spend a night at the lab where his dreams would be monitored by an EEG. He was awakened periodically by a research assistant so that transcripts of all his dreams could be taken for each night. The next morning the lab researchers would randomly select a packet from a set of similar packets, which contained an art print. The packet also included a description of a "scenario" suggested by the art work. This scenario usually entailed some sort of adventure Bessent would be taken on at the lab, and which hopefully his dreams would precognize.

This formidable task presented few problems for Bessent, who was able to dream about his forthcoming adventures quite regularly, though often in fragmented form. One night, for instance, he dreamt about an escaped patient in a hospital. The hospital theme was quite persistent and cropped up in more than one of his dreams that night. The reveries eventually became paranoid, hostile, and oppressive. The lab researchers were more than satisfied with the showing, for the target packet randomly chosen the next morning was based on Van Gogh's oppressive *Hospital Corridor at St. Remy*. This rather stark painting depicts a mental patient lingering in the corridor of a dimly lit, concrete corridor. The packet also instructed the experimenters to escort Bessent along a bleak corridor at Maimonides as part of the scenario they had in store for him.

The Maimonides researchers were so impressed by Bessent's performance that they designed a second experiment for him during the summer of 1970. Every other night over the course of several days Bessent was asked to dream about a slide sequence he would see the next day. The procedure for the experiments was roughly the same as was used during the 1969 tests. Bessent stayed at the lab so that his dreams could be monitored. Transcripts of his dreams were taken by waking him when he entered REM sleep. This project was just as successful as the earlier series. On the night of September 13, for instance, Bessent kept dreaming about blue skies, water, and birds. The bird motif seemed to be dictating the dreams, since imagery about our feathered friends showed up in three of his dreams for that night.

The target slides randomly chosen the next day revolved, as you might have guessed by now, around birds seen on land, water, and in the air. Bessent had similar success during fourteen of the sixteen sessions which constituted the experiment.

Now while all of this obviously demonstrates that ESP messages can influence our dreams, you might be wondering whether we can *use* dreaming as a technique for psychic development. This is, of course, the crucial issue with which this chapter is concerned, and the Maimonides work suggests that we can. If dreams normally serve as natural carriers of ESP information, then it should be somehow possible to tap our ESP potentials by programming them.

There is substantial evidence that this can be done, since several famous psychics have deliberately used dreaming as a key to the psychic world ... and especially to hone their precognitive gifts. J. W. Dunne, a British aeronautical engineer at the turn of the century, was probably the first to learn the trick. In his famous book *An Experiment with Time,* he recounts how he started paying close attention to his dreams after he dreamt about an argument he was having with a waiter. They were arguing about the correct time. Dunne subsequently discovered that the time he insisted it was in the dream matched the exact time he awoke from it. This alerted him to the possibility that dreams might offer a way by which to explore the nature of time. So over the next several years he kept a detailed log of his dreams and found that they often incorporated sights, scenes, and experiences apparently drawn from his upcoming week. This led him to believe that dreams represent a virtual window on our futures.

J. W. Dunne always insisted that he was not a psychic. He merely believed that he had discovered an odd quirk about the interrelation between time and dreaming. This is doubtful since several people tried to replicate Dunne's work, only to fail. It seems more likely that Dunne unintentionally programmed his dreams through his own intensive interest in precognition. This interest was coupled by his fascination with the whole concept of time (an interest that would occupy him for the rest of his life) and acted as a sort of breeding ground from which his psychic abilities burgeoned.

Similar discoveries hae been made more recently by Alan Vaughan, a former New York publishing house editor who became interested in the world of psychic phenomena in the 1960s. After quitting his job, he traveled widely and consulted extensively with both researchers and psychics in the United States and Europe. His interest in his own personal psychic development was piqued while he was residing in London, where he was able to attend psychic development classes conducted by Douglas Johnson, a renowned and talented British sensitive. These sessions stressed mental quietude, relaxation, openness to mental imagery, and a host of other mind-stilling exercises. They also served as the setting through which the members of the group would attempt to give psychic readings for one another, and Vaughan gradually found himself developing psychic abilities. It was through the art of dream control, however, that he found his most reliable source of psychic talent.

By examining and recording his dreams, Vaughan—like Dunne before him—found that psychic and precognitive information was often reflected in them. This led the enthusiastic investigator to see if he could deliberately manipulate his dreams in order to foretell the future. His procedure was to choose an upcoming public event, such as a space launch, program himself before he fell asleep to dream about it; record his dream or dreams in the morning; and then file it away or register it with another party before the event in question had transpired. By using this technique, Vaughan was able to discover that definite precognitive information about the forthcoming event would often come through.

Vaughan has gone on to diligently explore the nature of his dream powers. He eventually became a highly successful dream ESP subject at Maimonides Medical Center and often sends his predictions to the Central Premonitions Bureau in New York. This is an organization that regularly receives, registers, and documents predictions sent to them from all over the country. Vaughan has proven himself to be one of the Registry's most reliable psychic dreamers, and they have formally documented several of his precognitive dreams.

As a result of his self-observations and experimentations, Vaughan believes that anyone can develop psychic abilities and he actively encourages the use of dream control as a viable strategy. He has outlined several procedures for learning psychic ability through dream strategies in his book *The Edge of Tomorrow,* and regularly teaches seminars on psychic development in California, Arizona, Texas, and elsewhere.

TECHNIQUES FOR LEARNING DREAM ESP

In order to use your dreams as a royal road to ESP, you must first learn to recall them. People vary in their ability to remember their dreams. Some individuals claim virtually no dream recall, while others habitually remember one or even two a night. Psychologoists thought at one time that dream recall was an inborn or fixed character trait, and indeed people who are extroverted tend to report better dream recall than people who are introverted or neurotic. This view has gradually fallen by the wayside, though. Researchers interested in the psychology of sleep and dreaming have now learned that dream recall is at least partially a skill ... and as such, anybody can learn to enhance it.

The key to dream recall is practice and self-suggestion. By following the procedure outlined below you should note an improvement in your ability to remember your dreams within a relatively short time:

28

STEP NO. 1: REEVALUATE YOUR ATTITUDE TOWARD YOUR DREAMING LIFE.
You can't expect to remember your dreams unless you realize how important they can be to you. Spend a little time every day seriously questioning how you feel about your dreams until you have given up any misguided idea that dreams are unimportant or meaningless. It might help to read a couple of serious books on the practical use you can make of your dreams and how you can work to decipher their very personal messages.* A good primer on Jungian psychology, which views dreaming as a gateway to self-understanding, might also fit the bill. You must learn to respect the wisdom and value of your dreams if you expect them to work for you.

STEP NO. 2: BEGIN KEEPING A DREAM DIARY. As you reevaluate your attitude toward your dreams, you should also begin writing them down when you get up in the morning. The best way to proceed is to try recalling the dream from which you awoke, since we usually rouse from sleep during a REM cycle. Keep a pad or a tape recorder by your bed, and as soon you find yourself awake, write or record the dream in as much detail as possible. Try to re-experience it in your mind by closing your eyes and concentrating on it, since this will help you recall more of the dream. Now just don't ignore your dream after you have written it down. Try to understand its meaning or message by interpreting the symbols from which it has been constructed. You don't have to be a psychoanalyst to understand your dreams. Just think over various meanings the dream might have for you. When you chance on the correct one, you'll intuitively know it. This procedure will also help you gain a new respect for your dreams, while at the same time it will force you to focus at least part of your day on the importance of developing a rich dream life.

STEP NO. 3: COMMAND YOURSELF TO REMEMBER YOUR DREAMS WHEN YOU RETIRE. This simple procedure is amazingly successful for many people. When we retire we normally try to clear our minds, or we simply allow it to wander aimlessly until we are overtaken by sleep. However, it is also possible to use this pre-sleep stage more dynamically. Don't worry. This will not interfere with your sleep. The procedure is really quite simple. When you get into bed, just give yourself the command that you will remember your dreams. Keep giving yourself the command over and over as long as you can before you actually fall asleep. You might also give

*Two books I highly recommend are *Creative Dreaming* by Patricia Garfield (New York: Ballantine, 1979) and *Working with Dreams* by Dr. Montague Ullman and Nan Zimmerman (New York: Delacorte, 1979).

yourself the suggestion that you will wake up in the morning while you are still dreaming. Waking at such a time might put you in a better position to remember your dreams.

If none of these procedures works, there are more drastic measures you can use. Most people enter their first dreaming stage about 90 minutes after they fall asleep. You might set your alarm for this time, so that you will wake up during your first dream. Or you might set your alarm so that it wakes you a bit earlier than you usually arise. This might also cause you to awaken when you are still dreaming and when you can best remember the imagery.

Just paying attention to your dreams, recording them, analyzing them, and keeping a dream diary may actually serve as an end in itself. There is firm experimental evidence that people who report good dream recall tend to make good ESP subjects in the laboratory. Some lucky individuals find that observing the dreaming self automatically opens the way to psychic experiences. This is what J. W. Dunne apparently discovered. The more he examined his dreams, the more they became precognitive. So you might want to go over your dream diaries once a week to see if anything cropped up in them that seemed to foretell the future. Some of your dreams might have foreshadowed an event that happened the next day or during the week. You might also have to snoop around a bit. If you dreamt of someone you know, call them up and check out any information about them that may have manifested in your dream. This information might have been telepathically or precognitively received. I can recall a dream I had several years ago in which I lost my wallet while exploring a field late at night. I walked back to my car, only to find that it had been transformed into a Datsun. I don't drive a 240Z, but a good friend of mine does. This friend dropped by later that day and during our conversation mentioned that he had lost his wallet. That gave me the clue, so I asked him if by chance he had lost it the night before while walking around in a field. He was amazed!

On the other hand, some people intuitively know when they have had a psychic dream, since these dreams sometimes carry distinctive "signatures" along with them. A fellow parapsychologist I know well claims that dreaming in color, and not in black and white, tells him when a dream is paranormal. Yet another colleague of mine discovered that psychic information usually manifests in his dreams by forming unusual imagery sequences which insert themselves into a dream scenario that is proceeding along different lines. Many other people can simply recognize

30

psychic dreams by their distinctive emotional tone, vividness, or recurrence. There is no rule of thumb when it comes to identifying psychic dreams, though. Dreaming is a very personal matter and everyone will have to learn for him or herself how to tell if they are dreaming true. I, for instance, have had several precognitive dreams over the years. Never once have I been able to tell that a dream is precognitive until it has come to pass.

If you want to expand the psychic use of your dreams, however, you should learn to do more than merely remember them. You should seek to actually control them.

Dream control is one of psychology's hottest new areas of study. Years ago the psychological establishment would have laughed at the very idea that we could actually control, manipulate, or structure our dreams. Yet empirical research has now shown that dream control is a skill that can be learned through practice. By learning to control the basic content of our dreams, we can perhaps learn to program them for ESP. If it is possible to control what we dream *about*, it is reasonable to assume that we can program them to pick up, focus on, or refelct extrasensory signals and information by using similar techniques. Dr. Patricia Garfield, a brilliant psychologist living in San Francisco, has made a career out of the study of dream control and outlines several methods in her excellent book *Creative Dreaming*. These same procedures, with certain modifications, can be implemented for inducing psychic dreams as well.

The first step toward dream control is to convince yourself that you *can* influence your dreams. Unless you are committed to this belief, you won't have much luck learning the art. Once you have overcome any bias you might have about your ability to control your dreams, you can develop the skill by using any of the following techniques.

TECHNIQUE NO. 1: FOCUS ON A TOPIC YOU WISH TO DREAM ABOUT AND CONCENTRATE ON IT FULLY AS YOU RETIRE.   The key here is to immerse yourself mentally in some theme or topic and fall asleep while it is still in your mind. The theme should then gradually translate itself into your dreams. The main point is to really focus on the subject, explore it mentally, and try to keep it in mind as you actually fall asleep. I regularly employ this strategy for problem solving. If I am up against a problem in my life, I'll go over it while in bed, think about various courses of action I can take, and try to figure out what to do. Then I'll ask my subconscious to provide me with a dream that will shed light on the matter. I'm rarely disappointed.

31

TECHNIQUE NO. 2: GIVE YOURSELF SELF-SUGGESTIONS ABOUT YOUR DREAM TOPIC. Some people who have learned dream control consolidate their dream intentions into a simple phrase that they repeat over and over again while in bed until they fall asleep. This serves rather like a self-hypnotic suggestion. Something like, "Tonight I will dream about my friend so-and-so" should fit the bill. Focus on the phrase and repeat it like a mantra. It might also help to visualize the person or thing you want to dream about as intently as possible.

TECHNIQUE NO. 3: ENGAGE IN ACTIVITIES DURING THE DAY THAT ARE PERTINENT TO WHAT YOU WANT TO DREAM ABOUT. This procedure is similar to the first strategy outlined above, but you are now going to take your intention outside of your bedroom by making it part of your day's activities. For example, suppose you want to dream about a relative you haven't seen in a long time. Don't just think about him or her. Dig up some old photos of this person and look at them. Run some old home movies. Wear something once given to you by your relative. Maybe you should even take off during the day and visit a museum or park you once visited together. The whole key to this approach is to structure your day in such a way as to set up your dreams. Remember that dreams are usually formed by the experiences we undergo during the day. By using this procedure you are merely stacking the deck in your favor.

TECHNIQUE NO. 4: LEARN TO BECOME AWARE IN YOUR DREAMS. Some lucky individuals seem born with the knack of knowning that they are dreaming during the very course of their dreams. This phenomenon is called lucid dreaming, and represents a fascinating topic in its own right. There are several ways of inducing lucid dreams, but the art takes considerable practice. One of the simplest ways is to give yourself the suggestion that you will be alerted to the fact that you are dreaming by any incongruities that transpire in your nightime adventures. Most of us dream now and then of flying, floating, or engaging in some other physically impossible endeavor. If you give yourself strong suggestions when you go to sleep to be "on the lookout" for these incongruities, you might find yourself becoming aware during your dreams. Once you become aware that you are dreaming you can pretty well control your dreams. You can create any adventures for yourself that you like.

Now all of these strategies are basically learning devices. Dream control will become easier and easier the more you practice and eventually a casual suggestion at night should be enough to instigate the required control. And once you have learned to control and program your dreams, you can apply your talent to ESP. Any of the strategies that I have just listed can be used for ESP learning. For example:

TECHNIQUE 1. You might think about an upcoming event, such as an election, a space shot, or a vacation. Think about it intently from as many angles as you can and then give yourself the suggestion that you will dream about the future event. Be sure to write out your dreams as fully as possible the next day. Especially note any information that looks like it could be potentially precognitive. You might wish to repeat this procedure over several nights to see if any recurrent themes crop up. It is important that whatever you dream about should be important to *you*. Don't use any of these procedures flippantly.

TECHNIQUE 2. You might also wish to simplify matters by the use of a short command. Give yourself the suggestion, for example, that you will dream about a story that will appear on the front page of your local newspaper. Repeat this command over and over. Or you might wish to have a friend place a picture for you to experiment with in a sealed envelope. (For maximum security, the picture should be wrapped in tin foil which will prevent anyone seeing it through the envelope.) Keep this by your bed or under your pillow when you retire and give yourself the mental command that you will incorporate the picture into your dreams.*

TECHNIQUE 3. Follow the procedure you have outlined for the first strategy, but also incorporate activities pertinent to your upcoming dream in your daily routine. If you wish to precognize what will happen during an forthcoming space launch, for example, set yourself up all day by reading on the subject, visiting a science center or technology museum, or perhaps watching a science fiction movie. By engaging in this activities you will be programming yourself to have a precognitive dream. Residues from the day may serve as the vehicle for the precognitive information, which might revise what you have experienced to make it psychically meaningful.

TECHNIQUE 4. If you can learn to induce and control lucid dreams, all sorts of possibilities present themselves. It should be noted that, to date,

*Formal instructions for experimenting with pictorial targets will be outlined in the next chapter.

there is no experimental evidence that lucid dreaming is particularly psi-conducive. But relatively little research has so far explored a possible relationship. On the other hand, parapsychologists have collected tentative evidence that people who report psychic experiences also seem to report lucid dreams, so there might be some subtle relationship between these two phenomena. You can make psychic use of lucid dreaming by programming their contents to match any future event about which you might be trying to elicit information. *Live* the event you are trying to foresee. Or you might command your dreaming self, while you are dreaming, to present you with scenes from your own future.

Conjuring up meaningful figures in your dreams may also pave the way to your psychic potentials. Many mind dynamics courses train you to go deep within yourself and make contact with your "higher self" through meditation or self-hypnosis. It makes no difference whether you consider this as being your own inner helper, a guardian angel, a universal archetype, or even a witch's familiar! Researchers interested in clinical hypnosis have uncovered the very real existence of these inner guardians. Dr. E. R. Hilgard, a noted authority on hypnosis at Stanford University, calls this part of our minds the "hidden observer." This is a part of the unconscious that just sits back and watches everything that happens to us, takes stock of things, and seems to be a bit wiser than our waking selves appear to be. The hidden observer can be contacted through formal hypnosis, but we can also make contact with it ourselves through deep meditation and through our dreams. You might try to see if you can make contact with your hidden observer by programming your dreams and commanding him or her to appear. Do this repeatedly as you go to sleep. The hidden observer will probably manifest as a deceased relative, a religious figure, a wise old man, or even an animal. You will be able to recognize the hidden observer because it will appear as a form meaningful to you. If you succeed in making contact with this personage, or if such a character begins to appear consistently in your dreams, use this figure as a guide. Engage the figure as an active guide, and ask it about your future, or any problem preying on your mind. If the figure seems to be appearing regularly, you can start requesting before you go to sleep that he or she will bring along and convey any psychic information you are seeking.

This may sound awfully far-fetched, but it really isn't. A very good example of how a housewife discovered this strategy quite accidentally came by my desk while I was reviewing some manuscripts for *Fate* magazine, on whose staff I serve as consulting editor. The article dealt in part with a woman whose mother had died years before. The narrator was quite young at the time, and to console herself, she had learned to conjure up her mother in her dreams. She eventually learned to engage in all sorts of conversations with the dream figure, who often brought through stunningly accurate psychic information. Whenever a relative was sick or in danger, the dream figure would appear at the woman's beckoning and explain exactly what the future held. The dream figure also would appear to announce any upcoming deaths in the family.

Probably the most important thing to remember as you read this chapter is that you have a wide variety of dream strategies from which to choose should you want to use them as your personal road to ESP. You might wish to use different procedures for different purposes. Don't limit yourself!

The basic goal of using dreams as a key to your psychic potentials is that, eventually, your dreams may well begin to incorporate psychic information automatically. You may find that you don't have to program them to bring this information through. You will have trained your unconscious mind to use your dreams like psychic radar. This is what several psychics have learned. Alan Vaughan writes in his autobiographical *The Edge of Tomorrow,* that 25 percent of his dreams contain some sort of psychic (and especially precognitive) information.

Dreams can be a powerful tool in our search for a reliable method for psychic development. Learn to use them in every way you can.

References

Dunne, J. W. *An Experiment with Time.* London: Faber & Faber, 1927.

Hilgard, Ernest R. *Divided Consciousness.* New York: John Wiley, 1977.

Honorton, Charles. Reported frequency of dream recall and ESP. *Journal of the American Society for Psychical Research,* 1972, *66,* 369–74.

Palmer, John. A community mail survey of psychic experiences. *Journal of the American Society for Psychical Research.* 1979, *73,* 221–52.

Prasad, J. and Stevenson, Ian. A survey of spontaneous psychical experiences in school children of Uttar Pradesh, India. *International Journal of Parapsychology.* 1968, *10,* 241–61.

Rhine, Louisa. Frequency of types of experiences in spontaneous precognition. *Journal of Parapsychology,* 1954, *18,* 93–123.

Rhine, Louisa. Subjective forms of spontaneous psi experiences. *Journal of Parapsychology,* 1953, *17,* 79–114.

Rhine, Louisa. *ESP in Life and Lab.* New York: Collier Books, 1969.

Ullman, Montague, Krippner, Stanley, with Alan Vaughan. *Dream Telepathy,* New York: Macmillan, 1973.

Vaughan, Alan. *Patterns of Prophecy.* New York: Hawthorn, 1973.

Vaughan, Alan. *The Edge of Tomorrow.* New York: Coward, McCann, Geoghegan, 1982.

strategy 2

the role
of mental imagery

The Maimonides dream research produced perhaps the first major body of evidence alerting parapsychologists to the fact that ESP might be related to a certain state of mind more than to any other factor.

Not everybody remembers their dreams, though. So dreaming may not be the best way to gain access to our ESP talents. Not only that; dreams are often rather unclear. Transcribing them, trying to remember them in detail, and trying to decipher the symbolic language in which they communicate with us all can be a pain in the neck. So a few parapsychologists began trying to find even simpler techniques that just about *anyone* could use to tap their ESP abilities. One of these avenues was a direct offshoot of the Maimonides lab's dream research.

Charles Honorton was one of the dream lab's most enthusiastic young coexperimenters. He began his career as a research associate at the Foundation for Research on the Nature of Man in Durham, but transferred to New York in the mid-1960s and became one of Maimonides' most original thinkers and experimenters. Honorton eventually took charge of the lab when Ullman, swamped with administrative responsibilities, gradually withdrew from active involvement with the dream lab.

He expanded its operations over the next few years, retailored the lab's research, and took it in new and even more exciting directions.

While working at Maimonides, Honorton formulated the theory that ESP is intrinsically related to what might be called "internal attention states." He suggested that we don't usually experience ESP because we are just too busy dealing with the world around us. By not paying attention to what is going on in our minds, we thereby shut out any possible ESP impressions which might otherwise come to our attention. Having come to this conclusion, he set about trying to find a procedure which would induce his subjects to pay attention to the inner worlds of their mental images, daydreams, and introspections. The young researcher was extremely successful in his work and set the parapsychology scene ablaze in 1973 when he reported on an almost absurdly simple way of helping people gain access to ESP abilities which they probably didn't even know they had. Like most discoveries in parapsychology, however, this story, too, has a bit of a background.

For some years now, psychologists interested in visual perception have toyed with what is called "ganzfeld" stimulation. "Ganzfeld" is a German word which simply means "homogeneous field." These researchers were interested in discovering what psychological and visual effects would occur if a person were made to stare into a totally blank visual field. (For instance, staring pointedly at a white sheet would constitute a "ganzfeld.") Eventually a few of these psychologists began to wonder what would happen if these same subjects were made to listen to white noise (such as static of the sort you might pick up between radio stations) at the same time. What they found was interesting, to say the least. Most of their subjects began "hallucinating" or envisioning daydream-like images against the ganzfeld.

Now as I pointed out previously, ESP often manifests in the form of dreams, visions, and other types of mental imagery. So around 1972 Honorton realized that the ganzfeld might be used to help people have ESP experiences. In other words, he figured that these artificially induced daydream-like images might be experimentally used to "carry" ESP information from a sender to a receiver. He was soon able to prove his point in 1973 when he initiated a series of ingenious explorations into the ganzfeld setting.

For his first experiment, Honorton individually tested 30 nonselected subjects. Most of them were either lab or hospital staff members, while the others were chiefly happenstance visitors to the Maimonides center. Each subject was placed in the lab's soundproof booth, where he or she was comfortably seated in a soft reclining chair. In order to establish a ganzfeld setting, halved ping-pong balls were fastened over his or her eyes, cotton was wedged into any light leaks if the balls didn't fit tightly enough, and a red light was directed toward him. (The ping-pong balls diffused the illumination, so that all the subject could see was a perfectly uniform reddish visual field.) Next, earphones were placed over his head and the sound of monotonous ocean waves pitching to and fro was played through them. Each subject was instructed to relax and report over an intercom all the thoughts, images, and feelings he or she would experience over the next 35 minutes. While informed that an agent would send him a "message" by ESP at some point during the test, the subject was told not to try to guess or anticipate it.

While the subject was being set up in the ganzfeld, an agent was placed in another room. His job was to pick out a reel of viewmaster slides from a collection of several dozen and then "send" the pictures depicted on the reel to the subject for a five-minute period. Honorton, of course, wanted to see if his subject would incorporate the themes of the viewmaster slides into his mental imagery. After each session was over, the subject was given four reels to look at and asked to choose which one best matched what he had "seen" while in the ganzfeld.

Honorton's experiment was an outstanding success. Out of his first thirty subjects, close to half of them showed some indication of ESP while subjected to the ganzfeld. Quite often their mental imagery closely matched or reflected the viewmaster scenes which had been sent to them psychically. For example, one subject's target was a reel of U.S. Air Force Academy scenes. As the subject reported during part of her session:

> ... An airplane floating over the clouds ... Planes passing overhead ... Thunder now, angry clouds ... Airplanes ... Ultrasound ... A blaze of fire, red flames. A five-pointed star ... An airplane pointing down ...

And later she continued:

> A giant bird flying ... Six stripes on an army uniform, V-shaped. A face from the stripes. Now a V ... A mountain range snow-capped. Flying through the mountain ... The sensation of going forward very fast ... Machine gun. A ladder.

Another subject was telepathically sent a reel entitled "Birds of the World." At one point during the test he reported over the intercom, "I sense a large hawk's head in front of me, a profile. The sense of sleek feathers. Now it turns and flies away."

However, Honorton and his co-workers were in for a bit of a surprise when they sat down to seriously analyze their data. They found that sometimes their subjects correctly described the viewmaster scenes *before* the agent had started sending them, or even looking at them. These subjects didn't seem to be picking up their ESP impressions from the minds of the senders. Instead, it looked more as though their minds had picked up this information directly from the reels or had actually looked right into the future.*

But was it really the imagery induced by the ganzfeld that led to the success of Honorton's experiment? Or was the state of mind produced by sensory isolation the reason for the outcome of the project? Or could some other factor or combination of factors have come into play? Could the Maimonides workers simply have stumbled upon a crew of exceptionally good ESP subjects?

These were some of the questions that Honorton's original ganzfeld work raised and which were left unanswered. More research obviously had to be done.

The fact that ganzfeld tests are simple and inexpensive to run led several researchers at other parapsychology labs to attempt to replicate the Maimonides work under tighter experimental conditions after it had been officially reported in the April 1974 issue of the *Journal* of the American Society for Psychical Research. The results were sometimes mixed, but the ganzfeld has held up remarkably well.

Perhaps the most important of these replications was reported by William and Lendell Braud, two parapsychologists from Texas, in 1975. Their tests were conducted at the University of Houston and followed the Maimonides methods rather closely except for some important revisions. William Braud recruited twenty of his students (and others from the University) for the experiment. All of the subjects told the psychologist that they believed in ESP but, according to the Brauds, "none had had any striking psychic experiences prior to participating in the study." Ten of the students were given formal ganzfeld tests. They were taken into an isola-

*This discovery may sound a bit far-fetched, but in 1975 I worked at Maimonides myself and especially designed a precognition-ganzfeld experiment. I instructed my subjects to try and image about a picture that I would randomly choose only *after* their sessions were over. Although my experiment was not overwhelmingly successful, a few of my volunteers did seem able to peek into the future now and then. One subject described seeing Superman flying about some tall buildings during one of his sessions. The target picked for that test, which was chosen some five minutes after the experiment was over, depicted a dog in a Superman costume jumping through a window!

tion booth at the university, ping-pong balls were taped over their eyes, and they were asked to stare into a diffused white (not red) light. They simultaneously listened to undifferentiated static (technically called "white" or "pink" noise) over earphones and were instructed to report over an intercom all their thoughts and mental pictures. An agent was stationed in another room and tried to send the subject an ESP message based on a picture he chose from a target pool during the last five minutes of the test.

The ten other students acted as a control group. They were merely placed in the isolation booth and asked to sit quietly and to imagine what the target picture looked like. They were not subjected to formal ganzfeld stimulation but merely given the same instructions about relaxing and reporting their images that the experimenters had given their ganzfeld subjects.

After the test was over, each of the subjects were shown a series of six pictures. Only one, of course, was the actual target. The students were then asked to rate the pictures on a one-to-six scale. Their first, second, and third choices were to be those which had the greatest similarity to what they had seen while in the isolation booth.

The results of the test were rather startling. All ten of the ganzfeld subjects placed their targets in the upper half of their rankings. Yet the control subjects were typically unsuccessful at correctly identifying their targets, and often ranked them at the low end of the scale. The Brauds also interviewed their subjects after the test in order to determine whether the two groups differed on a host of other psychological factors which could have contributed to the gross difference in their success rate. They asked about their subjects' moods, attitudes towards the test, whether they liked their targets, and if they felt that their state of mind during the tests was conducive to the reception of ESP. The Brauds found no differences between the ganzfeld and control subjects on any of these items. Their tentative conclusion was, therefore, that it was indeed the state itself induced by the ganzfeld which had produced their success and no other factor.

However the Brauds were not absolutely convinced of this for several reasons. The whole theory behind the ganzfeld is that subjects do well because they are projecting their attention inwards and focusing their minds on their introspective experiences. But were Honorton's and the Brauds' subjects really doing this? "We would suggest," wrote the Brauds in their 1975 report issued in the *Journal* of the American Society for Psychical Research, "that some effort be devoted to the development of adequate indices of the degree to which subjects actually enter the hypnogogic state." The Brauds go on to point out that, just because a subject has been instructed to enter an altered state of consciousness, does not mean that he has actually done so!

An approach to this very problem was made by yet another researcher at another parapsychology laboratory. Dr. Carl Sargent, a psychologist at the University of Cambridge, began experimenting with the ganzfeld in 1978. He eventually conducted a series of highly successful experiments in which he gave his subjects "state report" scales as part of his tests. Each of his subjects was asked to determine how deeply he or she had entered into an "altered state" during his/her ganzfeld experience. Sargent was able to determine that those subjects who reported a severe alteration of consciousness during their ganzfeld exposure did much better than those who remained relatively unaffected by the isolation.

So once again it appears that it is the state of consciousness induced by the ganzfeld that gives one access to his ESP potential and not some other X factor.

The ganzfeld is today still one of the most popular and consistently successful procedures parapsychologists have discovered which helps people gain access to their ESP potential. It is certainly remarkable that all of the Brauds' initial students succeeded at demonstrating ESP although none of them could recall ever having a conscious ESP experience. This certainly indicates that ESP might well be a learnable or developable talent. And the ganzfeld does seem to be fairly reliable. This point was emphasized by Honorton himself when he spoke about his research to an international conference on parapsychology that convened in Paris in August 1977. The young Maimonides researcher pointed out that between 1974-77 he and his colleagues had conducted eight series of ganzfeld tests. Seven of these had been successful. He went on to point out that the ganzfeld procedure had also been tested by researchers at some ten other laboratories. Seven of these had been extremely successful.

"We now have something to build on," reported Honorton when he discussed ways that ESP might be made more reliable.

If we add Sargent's careful work to this list, one can see that the ganzfeld procedure has been remarkably successful as a "psi-conducive" state-of-mind induction technique.

But why should the ganzfeld be so efficacious in helping ordinary and very unpsychic people receive ESP impressions so consistently? There are a number of answers to this question.

To begin with, we live in a fast-moving world which keeps our minds and bodies going at a frantic pace. We really don't have much time to pay attention to our innermost thoughts and feelings. We're just too preoccupied with our work, worries, finances, love lives, and business dealings to bother about what's going on in our heads. In the ganzfeld we do, though. While sitting comfortably and cut off from disturbing sights and sounds which bombard us constantly during the course of an average day, we can be alone with our thoughts. It may well be that, while in this state, we can *allow* ESP impressions to surface into our conscious minds. We can tap our own inner potentials in a way impossible to us in our day-to-day bustling lives.

Secondly, the mind apparently becomes starved for stimulation while in the ganzfeld. It can't hear or see anything, so it becomes vigilant for stimulation. In other words, our minds start wandering about *looking* for something to stimulate it. Any detectable ESP messages might just fit the bill.

The results of Honorton's ganzfeld research also hold out a very special promise to those of us interested in the possibility that someday we might be able to teach people to be psychic. I once balked at this idea. But I don't any more … and for a very good and personal reason. So let me engage in a bit of autobiography for a moment.

Frankly, I'm about as psychic as a silver dollar. While I've had my share of little nonconsequential psychic experiences, I certainly don't consider myself psychic in the least. But I do know that I have the potential locked within me. Unfortunately, I don't happen to have the key handy. Now, I was one of Honorton's original ganzfeld subjects. I got roped into the test one day in the summer of 1973 at the Maimonides lab while en route to another lab in North Carolina. The ganzfeld work had just been initiated at the time, and Chuck wanted to run me as a subject. I warned him that I was a lousy ESP subject and suggested to him *not* to use me. But he insisted, so I acquiesced.

As a ganzfeld subject, I was a complete flop just as I knew I would be. My mental imagery had nothing to do with the target pictures whatsoever. I even got so bored during the test that I peeked under the ping-pong balls now and then at my watch to see how much longer I would have to endure that damnable red light.

However, in 1975 the Southern California Society for Psychical Research in Beverly Hills asked me to take a one-year position as their Director of Research and to institute a research program. I decided to explore the ganzfeld in order to isolate some of the variables that might be affecting it, and because it was the hottest development on the psychic scene. A grant given me by the New York-based Parapsychology Foundation helped considerably.

I initially spent several weeks at Maimonides to carry out some of my own research. This allowed me to consult with the developers of the technique before implementing some of my programs back in Los Angeles. I also began using myself as a subject every so often just to get a better idea about what *my* subjects were going through. I eventually even began to like the ganzfeld and the sense of relaxation that accompanies the state, and acted as a subject in some of the Maimonides Center's own research. And now and then my mentation gradually began to match, though only vaguely, the ESP targets sent to me by my agent. But then something happened which really startled me and got me thinking about how the ganzfeld might be used for ESP training.

I arrived in New York from Los Angeles early one morning and went directly to the lab. Since I always take night flights to the east coast, I was spent by the time I arrived at the Maimonides Center. I had missed a night's sleep and was suffering jet lag to boot. Only about an hour after I had arrived, though, Chuck asked me if I would act as a subject in a practice ganzfeld session. It was being arranged to teach a new lab worker how to run the test and manage all the recording equipment. Of course I agreed.

That ganzfeld session was different from any other in which I had ever participated. I was tired ... almost sleepy and dozing ... and, as I looked at the red field in front of me, brilliant images kept flashing in front of my eyes. I saw an African scene, with a pool of water surrounded by tall grass. I even thought I saw an animal near the pool but wasn't sure. Toward the end of the session, I saw, in a stunning vision, a bird-like figure with outstretched wings eerily silhouetted before a pale moon.

This imagery was mixed in with a lot of random thoughts, visionings, and mental "noise." Yet these themes—which were ultimately related to the target picture—seemed to eke into my random thoughts now and then with special persistence.

The following is a transcription of what I reported during the 30 or so minutes I was subjected to the ganzfeld. Italicized passages relate to the target picture which I had not yet seen.

I can see two people trying to hail a taxi cab late at night, but the cab looks like the shape of ... two pieces of toast on a plate. Two people on a street at night. Muggers or something. I hear the words "your money or your life."

Wearing white as a safety against muggers in the night. Now I see an island and a castle plushly decorated. Two women, one in a white maid's outfit. I see a courtyard again, something rather medieval.

A pond with a lot of green grass, a tree in foreground. And I see some people there in the background. A possum dangling by its feet, its body hanging on its back and seems like it's dangling from the limb of a tree.

I see a man talking or pointing to something with his hand. Again an automobile of a golden color.

By this time I had been in the ganzfeld for about ten minutes. The imagery had followed a predictable pattern. Notice my first images were basically *threatening* and *dark* scenes, which finally gave way to more specific images of a night scene in the jungle. The first part of this session thus had a strong thematic or atmospheric relationship to that part of the session more pertinently related to the target.

After several fleeting images, which went by so quickly that I could barely grasp them, my mind returned to the nature scene I had begun to describe above:

I see a forest again. There's a clearing in front of it. There might be some animal there again.

I see a large bird like a vulture against a blue sky. White clouds. Very solitary. That was very strong.

I see a clock with its second hand going backwards. Now my whole visual field is becoming like a huge diamond—sparkling.

After the session was over, I was especially struck by the image of the bird. I explained to my experimenter that the mental image was of a bird or bird-like creature hovering with its wings *outstretched* against a *bright circular white field* (the moon?). This image had flashed into my mind suddenly; so suddenly, in fact, that it shocked me!

I was flabbergasted when I eventually saw the picture which had been the ESP target for the session. Just about all of this spontaneous imagery matched portions of the very unusual picture my agent had been trying to transmit to me. It depicted a forest scene, centering on a sparkling pool surrounded by tall grass towards which a leopard is seen creeping. Up in the sky, a moon partially hidden by white clouds illuminates the scene. A bat, suspended in air with outstretched wings, hovers beneath it. A snake (not an opossum) is dangling from a tree in the forefront of the picture.

My session had been an outstanding success, and my reputation as a "lemon" ESP subject came to a sudden end.

But why, I thought, had this session been so successful while my other attempts in the ganzfeld had usually failed miserably? The answer soon dawned on me. During the session I had been very relaxed, almost asleep. I had paid particular attention to those images which had appeared before my eyes just before I would have normally dozed off. Had I not had to verbally report these images over an intercom, I probably would have crashed out right in the isolation booth. Could these images (which are properly called *hypnagogic* images), I thought, be my own personal road to ESP?

When I returned to Los Angeles a few weeks later, I was determined to find out. Each day I tested myself. I would lay down on my living room couch and read until my eyes became a bit blurry and I felt groggy. I would then place a picture sealed inside a manila envelope (from a group of fifty I have) next to my head and try to doze off. (Since these pictures had been selected and placed in their envelopes by a colleague of mine, even I didn't know what any of them depicted.) At that time, I would also give myself the mental suggestion to "look into the envelope" as I began to doze. As soon as I began seeing hypnagogic imagery before falling fully asleep, I would rouse myself, write down what I saw, and then open the envelope.

Some of my successes were quite concise, in which the basic themes of the pictures seemed to be consolidated and simplified into a single mental image. One picture, for instance, depicted an old man wearing a blue coat and hat walking by a river with a dog and a boy by his side. My mental image was simply of a Napoleon-type character with a black hat. Another picture was of an Indian shaman staring out at the viewer and wearing a ram's head mask and holding two rattles. My mental and clairvoyant image of this target was simply of a negro figure looking directly outwards. And when a target was two children wearing red shawls, I saw a teenager with a red bandana around his head.

These experiments were very informally done, so I certainly am not presenting them in order to "prove" ESP, or to try to convince you that I'm psychic … which I really don't think I am. The only point I am trying to make is that, through my exposure to the ganzfeld, it seems that I had begun to "learn" ESP. My experiences during those sensory isolation sessions seemed to be helping me identify what *kind* of mental images are most likely to be psi-mediated ones. I was learning to isolate them from the more random thoughts and images that were interplaying with them. In essence this was some sort of learning process.

A similar discovery has recently been made by Dr. Carl Sargent as part of his research at the University of Cambridge. He discovered during the course of his work that many of his best subjects seemed to get better and better at the ganzfeld. He even ran an experiment with people who had already gone through the procedure, and compared how they did on a subsequent test with a set of naive subjects. The experienced subjects easily out-performed the newcomers on the ESP test. One of Sargent's star subjects even developed his own personal "learning strategy." He would sit in the ganzfeld and deliberately generate mental images until a random image just popped into his head. These images, he determined, were usually psychic messages.

So while my original ganzfeld experiences did not necessarily help me gain access to my ESP potential, they did help me uncover and learn a way I actually could.

Many parapsychologists, other than Honorton and myself, have discovered that mental imagery, which often occurs near sleep or during meditation, is a natural carrier of ESP information. *So to tap our ESP abilities, it looks as though we simply need to learn how to visualize or at least observe our mental imagery.* By learning *how* to visualize, can one also learn how to be psychic? The answer seems to be yes.

One visualization technique which is becoming increasingly popular among clinical psychologists is called "guided imagery." This is a procedure by which a psychologist can help his client learn how to daydream. The basic techniques of this procedure were first developed by Dr. Hanscarl Leuner of the University of Göttingen. As a psychologist, he found that "guiding" his patients through specially structured daydreams had considerable therapeutic value. These daydreams usually involved conflicts the patients were trying to resolve, and the imagery often helped them confront and understand their problems. Leuner would even go so far as to take his patients on imaginary trips, such as following a river to its source, walking through a meadow, etc. The patient would often be asked to elaborate on what he was seeing or experiencing during these trips. Other psychologists working with these procedures have learned that guided imagery fantasies can help patients gain access to deep realms of the unconscious and even control deep-seated feelings and emotions.

But can guided imagery also help people gain access to ESP powers? Some tentative findings along these very lines were presented at the

17th Annual Convention of the Parapsychological Association (held at St. John's University in Jamaica, New York, in August 1974) by Edward Charlesworth of the University of Houston.

For his experiment, Charlesworth had each of his subjects undergo what he calls an "imaginary dream." At the onset of the experiment, each subject was given relaxation exercises to carry out. These included muscle relaxation procedures and deep breathing exercises. Once the subject was relaxed, he was told to imagine a dream he might have had as a child. He was instructed to think about getting out of bed, walking through his bedroom closet, and into a grassy meadow. From there he was guided through the meadow, up and through a forest, onto a mountain, and down to a beach. At each stage of the imaginary dream, the subject was asked to envision something unusual. For example, if the subject were being led through a mountain, he would be told to imagine something that one would not normally expect to see there.

During this imaginary trip, an ESP sender was situated in another room at the University of Houston. Each time the subject was asked to imagine an unusual object or scene, the agent's job was to open a specially prepared envelope and stare at the picture inside. Of course, Charlesworth hoped that the subject would incorporate the picture viewed by the agent into the scene he was envisioning.

Like the ganzfeld, this technique, too, was quite successful. Although Charlesworth's experiment has not yet been replicated by other parapsychologists, his research at least indicates that many of us might be able to use common daydreaming to help us receive ESP messages.

By this time, you might have noticed a common thread which links together Honorton's ganzfeld work, Charlesworth's guided imagery experiment, the Maimonides dream studies, and even my own imagery exercises. All these techniques seem to work best if the subject is as relaxed as possible. If one is looking for a solution to the ESP mystery this certainly might be a critical clue. Physical relaxation might just be the simplest way yet known by which to help people develop ESP. This is a theme which we will explore more fully in the next chapter.

But, you might ask, what good is ESP if one has to go through such an elaborate ritual just to gain access to it?

My answer is that such procedures as the ganzfeld and guided imagery techniques may actually be best used as learning devices. Once a person has had enough success with these tools, perhaps he or she might be able to dispense with them altogether as we try to use our ESP.

This possibility came to my attention forcibly in 1980 during yet another trip to the Maimonides lab. By this time, the lab had moved out of the hospital and had been reinstituted as the Psychophysical Research Laboratories in Princeton, New Jersey. No sooner had I arrived at the lab than one of their researchers, a very attractive young doctoral student from City College in New York, asked me to participate in one of her studies. I wasn't the least bit in the mood to undergo a half hour of sensory isolation. I was excited about getting back to the lab and was rather hyperactive. I didn't think I would be able to enter an altered state of consciousness deep enough to demonstrate ESP. But Nancy insisted and I agreed. A friend of mine at the lab acted as my agent.

I was extremely alert throughout my ganzfeld session. I never found myself slipping into an altered state or becoming drowsy. Mental images didn't appear before my eyes very facilely and it often felt as if I were deliberately conjuring them up. But images of flowers kept nagging at my attention. At one point I even envisioned a single large sunflower. "I see a sunflower," I reported over the intercom. "A big, ugly sunflower." When the test came to a close some minutes later, I could hardly wait to get out of the booth!

After Nancy had read my mentation report back to me, she showed me several pictures and asked me to choose the one which had been the target. One of them was a beautiful close-up photograph of a daisy or sunflower. Both Nancy, who did not yet even know herself which picture was the target, and I immediately agreed that this must have been the target. It was.

I was rather impressed by this success since I had not really felt any change in my mental state during the test. This indicated that perhaps I had become sensitive to ESP through my ganzfeld experiences and had now become able to gain access to it more readily. In other words, the ganzfeld had "tuned me" into my own ESP capabilities. This idea was reinforced several months later when Carl Sargent reported on some new findings he had made. Sargent had been retesting some of his previously successful ganzfeld subjects and had made a fascinating discovery. The subjects were still performing well on his tests, but were no longer report- ing an intense alteration in consciousness as part of it. Sargent's findings thus tie in remarkably well with my own experience.

Once again I want to emphasize that I am not being auto- biographical because I think I'm psychic, or want to impress you with my extrasensory prowess. I have drawn upon my personal experiences because I am definitely *not* psychic, nor probably ever will be since I have no great desire to develop personal psychic powers. But I have become sensitive to ESP impressions as a result of my ganzfeld experiences. And if I can develop such powers even to a limited degree, then *anybody* should be able to! Before I began studying the whole area of altered states of consciousness I was very opposed to that school of thought which believed that we all possess ESP and can develop it. I have now been forced to change my mind. The key may indeed be mental imagery.

LEARNING TO GENERATE AND CONTROL MENTAL IMAGERY

Just as many people have a difficult time remembering their dreams, we all vary in our ability to generate, hold, and control mental pictures. Psychologists have long known that we code information and store it into our memory banks by the use of two strategies. These consist of a visual code and a verbal code. Most people tend to think predominantly in either mental pictures or verbally, each process relating to one or the other of these codes. Of course, we all rely on both these systems. Which code we use for each piece of information we are storing or retrieving depends on what we are trying to remember, but some of us tend to *prefer* visualization while others tend to be verbalizers. Whether or not each of our individual "cognitive styles" is invariable is a point of contention among cognitive psychologists. There is, nonetheless, some evidence that one can learn to at least enhance one's imagery capacities.

This issue is very pertinent to the study of ESP, especially if you are trying to develop the ability. If you don't happen to be a strong visualizer, perhaps using mental imagery as a strategy by which to learn ESP will not be your best bet. There is some evidence that people with different cognitive styles actually have different forms of ESP experiences. It should also be noted that whether or not strong visualizers are also good ESP subjects is a moot point, since the research findings in this area are mixed. However, learning to use mental imagery may well be an excellent way of gaining access to ESP information, and many psychics of the past and present have freely used it.

The first step in applying imagery strategies to ESP learning is to determine whether you are a visualizer or a verbalizer. If you are a naturally gifted visualizer, you may not really need to spend much time learning how to enhance and control mental pictures; you may already possess this ability. If you are a verbalizer by nature, though, you are going to have to spend some time opening your mind to the fascinating world of mental imagery. You can learn for yourself if you are more prone to imagery or verbalization through the following short tests, which I have adapted from a standard questionnaire that is widely used in psychology to determine cognitive style. The test upon which the following material is drawn is rather long and complex, so I have simplified it for home use. Analyzing the results of the formal questionnaire is also somewhat complex, so I have also simplified the procedure accordingly.

You should begin by answering the following questions on a five-point scale: give yourself five points if you strongly agree with the statement, four if you agree, three if you neither agree nor disagree, two if you disagree, and one if you strongly disagree:

1. I usually form a mental picture of a scene I am reading about.
2. I can often use my mental pictures to solve problems.
3. Sometimes I daydream so vividly that I can actually experience the scene.
4. I feel I have a vivid imagination.
5. I can easily envision moving objects in my mind.
6. I can create a mental image of any object suggested to me.
7. I can easily visualize the faces of people I know or am familiar with.
8. I can envision scenes from my past experiences with no difficulty.
9. I believe in the saying that a picture is worth a thousand words.
10. I can add numbers together by imagining them written on a blackboard or on a piece of paper.
11. I can sometimes recall something I have read by mentally reconstructing the page on which it was written.
12. I have very vivid dreams.
13. I learn better by watching a demonstration than through written instructions.
14. Before falling asleep I often see pictures before my eyes.
15. My thinking often consists of mental pictures or images.

Now add up your total points and divide by the number of questions. See on which side of the mean (2.5) you fall. If you have averaged 3.5 or more, this signifies that you tend to be a strong imager. If you scored below the mean, you may be more of a verbalizer.

To double check your cognitive style, you should now answer the series of questions listed below and also scale them on a five-point scale of agreement:

1. I do not have a problem expressing myself verbally.
2. I find writing easy.
3. I enjoy rephrasing my thoughts in a variety of ways both when I write and speak.
4. I enjoy learning new words and increasing my vocabulary.
5. When I am reading, I find myself more critical of the writing style than the actual content.
6. When I hear or read a word, several other words come to mind.
7. I usually don't have to revise what I write since I tend to express myself well in my first draft.
8. I am good at creating puns.
9. I never use mental pictures when I am trying to solve a problem.
10. I cannot recall what some public figures look like, even though I may have seen pictures of them.
11. I believe that people should pay more attention to the manner in which they express themselves.
12. I enjoy word games and crossword puzzles.
13. I find it difficult to form mental pictures.
14. I don't tend to form mental pictures of people, places or scenes I am reading about.
15. My daydreams tend to be indistinct and hazy.

Once again add up your total and see if it falls above or below the mean of 2.5. Also compare your scores on this subtest to the one you have computed on your use of mental imagery. Is there is a noticeable difference between them? If there is, this should indicate that you tend to rely on either an imagery or verbal code more consistently. Please remember, though, that the above profiles represent only a very rough way of determining anything about your cognitive style. A proper and more authoritative questionnaire gauging the exact dynamics of your coding strategies would take a test twice as long and much more complex methods of statistical appraisal. The above subtests have only been designed to give you an approximate *idea* of your imagery skills and potentials.

If you scored very highly on the imagery scale, you may not need to learn to improve your imagery capacities. If you score around the average or lower, though, you might wish to proceed with the following exercises, which are designed to help you increase your capacity for controlling and generating mental imagery. These programs and exercises are based on a manual for imagery enhancement currently being used by some parapsychologists specifically for ESP training. They were first developed by Leonard George, a psychologist at the University of Western Ontario, who is interested in the relationship between ESP and mental imagery. He developed these exercises based on his own familiarity with different metaphysical schools and disciplines that emphasize the power of mental imagery. His unpublished manual was put in its present form while he was a research associate at the Institute for Parapsychology in Durham, North Carolina.*

The total course outlined by Mr. George includes several weekly sessions led by an instructor, as well as a series of homework exercises the student is expected to practice before attending the next class. For the purposes of the present book, I have adapted and modified these procedures for solitary practice without formal instruction.

Since the ability to generate mental imagery is partly a result of our base arousal level, any attempt to practice generating or controlling mental imagery should be prefaced by some sort of relaxation procedure. This can be an informal "cooling down" you go through as you begin each of your practice sessions, or you can formalize it into a ritual. You might wish to just lie down for awhile, try to clear your mind, and then proceed with your imagery exercises. Or you may prefer to prepare a tape for yourself to play at the beginning of a session. The suggestions that Mr. George uses to teach imagery enhancement are geared to provide mental quietude more than formal muscular relaxation:

> Pull your attention away from the various everyday concerns and problems you may have, and focus on the sensations in your body right now. You can feel the positions of the muscles, and activities of the organs ... Focus on these feelings, and relax ... Breathe deeply, and naturally ... In a few moments, I will ask you to imagine something as vividly as possible. Don't strain at this, just let it happen. I'll ask you to imagine that a gentle warm energy is slowly flowing into your body through your toes. This energy will slowly flow up your body, spreading through your limbs, and wherever you feel this sensation of warmth, all of the muscles in that area will relax completely ... You can feel this gentle energy flowing into your feet, through your toes ... It reaches the backs of your feet, and is flowing into your ankles ... All of the muscles are completely relaxed ... You can feel the soft, relaxing sensation flowing up the backs of the legs, to the backs of your knees ... Up the fronts of your legs, to the knees, and all of the muscles are loosened and

---

*The entire and detailed unpublished manual can be obtained directly from Leonard George, c/o the psychology department of the University of Western Ontario. Mr. George has to date conducted only one experiment testing the efficacy of these procedures for enhancing ESP. His results indicated that subjects who spent the longest time practicing the imagery exercises tended to score best on subsequent ESP tests.

relaxed ... Around the knees and the backs of the knees, the muscles are warm and relaxed ... The warm sensation is flowing up the backs of your upper legs ... Up the fronts of your upper legs ... Muscles are relaxed ... Throughout the pelvic region, the gentle energy washes away all tension ... The warm sensation flows into your lower back, relaxing the muscles ... Into your abdomen ... Your breathing is loosened, very free ... Warmth flows into your upper back, to the bottom of the back of your neck ... Muscles relaxed ... Soft energy flows throughout your chest, up to the base of the throat ... Warm sensation moves into your shoulders ... to your upper arms ... elbows ... forearms ... wrists ... hands ... right to the tips of all your fingers, and all of the muscles are very relaxed ... Warm, relaxing feeling spreads up the back of your neck ... to the back of your head, and expands across your scalp ... Warm energy flows into your throat ... Your jaw is relaxed ... Your forehead is warm and relaxed ... Your cheeks are relaxed ... Finally, let go of your eyes, muscles of your eyes are completely relaxed ...

You can use these suggestions to generate ideas from which to make your own tape, or you can read them into a tape verbatim.

The formal techniques for learning to generate and intensify mental imagery can be broken down into several sessions in which you teach yourself to gain better control over more and more complex imagery. You should not begin experimenting with any of the intermediate or advanced strategies until you have mastered the basics. The basic strategies are as follows:

Exercise No. 1

1. Relax your body and mind.
2. Look at a red square propped up in front of you on a chair for a few breaths. Then, as you inhale, feel as if the color has entered your head. Now close your eyes and see the color vividly before your mind's eye.
3. Hold the color for three breaths. As you take each breath, see it become more and more vivid.
4. As you exhale on the third breath, feel the color leave your head. You may then open your eyes.
5. Repeat steps 2 to 4 for a series of other colors, using the following order: orange, yellow, green, light blue, dark blue, violet, white. Then work through the colors in reverse order.
6. Repeat the entire cycle (red to white to red) two to four times in succession.

Exercise No. 2

1. Relax your body and mind.

2. Close your eyes and visualize the outline of a circle against a grey back-ground. Hold this for a short while.
3. Repeat step 2 using a triangle.
4. Repeat step 2 using a square.
5. Repeat step 2 using a five-pointed star.
6. Repeat step 2 using a six-pointed star.
7. Now see if you can visualize a circle, then watch as it changes into a triangle, then a square, and so on, until you have a six-pointed star. Allow the outlines to change very slowly, and carefully attend to these changes.
8. Now, starting with the six-pointed star, observe it slowly evolve back through the shapes to the circle. Watch the circle shrink into a point, then disappear.
9. Repeat steps 7 and 8 several times.

Exercise No. 3

1. Relax your body and mind.
2. Visualize an apple and hold the image for about thirty seconds.
3. Repeat step 2 using an orange.
4. Repeat step 2 using a banana.
5. Repeat step 2 using a green leaf.
6. Repeat step 2 with a light blue bird.
7. Repeat step 2 using a bowl of blue ink.
8. Repeat step 2 using an eggplant.
9. Repeat step 2 using an unbroken egg.
10. This exercise may be repeated with any simple colored object with which you are familiar.

This entire set of exercises should be repeated at least once a day. For best results you might do them in the morning and afternoon and then when your retire at night.

The following are intermediate strategies:

Exercise No. 1

1. Relax your body and mind.
2. Examine the red square for a few breaths as you did in the first series. Then, as you inhale, feel the color enter with your breath, and go down to the base of your spine and into the genital area. Feel it hovering there like a bright star.
3. Hold this image for three breaths. Notice any feelings that may accompany this visualization procedure.
4. As you exhale on the third breath, see the color leave your body along with the breath.

5. Repeat steps 2 to 4 for other colors in the following order:
   An orange light going down into the abdomen an inch below the navel.
   A yellow light going down into the solar plexus (beneath the rib cage).
   A green light going down into the heart.
   A light blue light going down into the upper chest.
   A dark blue light going down into the throat.
   A violet light going into the center of the brain.
   A white light going to the top of the head.
6. Go through this cycle two to four times.

Exercise No. 2

1. Relax your body and mind.
2. Visualize a simple unadorned teapot. Watch it slowly rotate around once, and carefully examine the various views.
3. Now visualize the pot slowly tipping, so that you can see the top. Continue to move it in this direction, so you can see the other side, then the bottom, and finally the original side again. Be prudent about noting all the details of the images.
4. Try this exercise with other simple objects familiar to you. It may be helpful to rotate the actual object in your hands first, and then close your eyes and do the exercise.
5. Imagine that you are approaching the object, and getting inside it and looking around.

Exercise No. 3

1. Relax your body and mind.
2. Imagine a red circle slowly rolling into the view of your mind's eye from one side, and a yellow circle entering from the other side.
3. Watch as the circles slowly roll into each other, forming a single orange circle, which then rolls away.
4. Imagine a red circle and a blue circle, which merge to form a violet circle.
5. Imagine a yellow circle and a blue circle, which merge to form a green circle.
6. Now imagine this merging process in reverse ... e.g. an orange circle dividing into red and yellow. Try this for the other colors.
7. Repeat steps 2 to 5 several times.
8. What do you see when a yellow circle, a red circle, and a blue circle overlap? The overlap should occur slowly, so that you can observe the details.

Carry out this set of exercises once or twice a day. Mr. George suggests that you do not become discouraged if you have difficulty with these exercises at first. Remember that you are developing a new skill and you will have to practice to perfect it.

These are advanced strategies:

Exercise No. 1

1. Relax your body and mind.
2. Close your eyes and visualize a bright red square.
3. After several seconds, place an orangé square above the red one.
4. Continue to place colored squares above each other in the standard sequence: red to white, so that they form a rainbow pillar in your mind's eye. Hold this for as long as possible without straining. Experience the array of colors shining on you.
5. When your attention wanders, or when the image fades, go back to visualizing the red square, and build the pillar up again. There may be a tendency to build it rapidly. Do not allow this. Always leave several-second intervals between new squares, during which time you should admire your "mindwork."
6. Spend five to ten minutes on this exercise. Don't worry if you can't get beyond three or four squares. Just proceed at your own rate.

Exercise No. 2

1. Relax your body and mind.
2. Close your eyes, and imagine that you are seeing a red balloon floating at the ceiling of the room.
3. Watch in your mind's eye as this balloon slowly rolls around the room, encountering the walls, furniture, and various objects. Attend to the various colors and positions of the objects in the room.
4. Try this with several different familiar places besides your home. Try to gradually increase your awareness from the space immediately adjacent to the balloon to the wider context of the room, somewhat like a zoom effect in reverse. Be sure to proceed slowly. Be aware of details.

Exercise No. 3

1. Relax your body and mind.
2. Visualize a golden crown studded with multicolored gems. Maintain this image for several seconds.
3. Stop "holding" the image, but remain attentive to it. Let it just linger in your consciousness. If the image disappears immediately, or if you instantly drift from it, visualize the crown again, hold it, then let it go.
4. Suggest to yourself that as you watch it, the crown will change into something else (but perhaps not immediately). Allow this to happen, and follow it passively, keeping your attention directed to the image that forms.
5. Follow the spontaneous changes of the image for a few minutes. Try to stay focused so that your experience is vivid, but do not try to direct or hold the image.
6. Try the same procedure with other evocative images, such as a boulder, a rocket, a meditator, a tree and so on.

These are complex strategies:

Exercise No. 1

1. Relax your body and mind.
2. This exercise is a little different from the previous color exercise. Progressively visualize a sequence of colors from red, to yellow, green, light blue, dark blue, violet, and white. Try to "hear" a musical tone accompanying each color. Hear the deepest tone you can imagine for red, and then use progressively higher pitches for each successive color.
3. Proceed until you reach white and hear a very high but pleasant hum, just on the verge of inaudibility.
4. Repeat this exercise two to four times.

Exercise No. 2

1. Relax your body and mind.
2. Imagine that your body is filled with a soft, inky blackness.
3. Visualize the appearance of a bright white sphere about an inch in diameter in the region of your heart. Let the sphere float to the top of your head, where it pops out.
4. At this point, try to merge your point of view with that from the sphere. Look around the room from the sphere's perspective and simply regard your body as another object in the room.
5. Drift out of the room along with the sphere (through a wall or ceiling, if you like). Try traveling to a destination that interests you, and explore it. Attend to the vivid images as you fly to the destination and look around.
6. Return to your body. Reenter through the top of your head, go down to the heart, and begin to feel your body again.

After you have practiced these exercises and feel that you now have some control over your mental imagery, you can begin testing yourself for ESP. The best way to proceed is with the use of pictures sealed in envelopes. It would be best to ask a friend or relative to prepare these for you, so that you will remain totally unfamiliar with the contents. The pictures should be aesthetically pleasing, as different as possible, and relatively simple. Each picture should have a distinct theme or focus on a central object, figure, or person. Each picture should also be wrapped in tin foil or placed in a folder made of black construction paper and then sealed in a manila envelope. You should begin with a set of six.

There are three ways you can now test yourself. One procedure relies on a specific mental command technique, while the other two allow you to free associate with the target.

The Mental Command Technique*

This technique emphasizes your ability to focus directly onto the ESP target and drag it into consciousness by the use of mental imagery. You can test yourself by following the steps listed below. It is highly advisable to practice in a room isolated from the rest of your home, where you are not likely to be disturbed.

1. Lie down or sit in a comfortable chair with one of the target pictures close at hand.
2. Relax yourself through any means you find efficient.
3. Visualize a neutral object by closing your eyes and holding the image stationary.
4. While maintaining the image, give yourself the suggestion—or instruct your subconscious mind—to show you the picture inside the envelope.
5. Now wait passively until the image you have created either changes into something else, or until other images start spontaneously popping up and displacing it.
6. If the image you receive is fragmented, give yourself the further suggestion that the image will appear in a more complete form.
7. Wait passively but attentively until the image reforms as a more complete picture.
8. Analyze your reaction to the image. Be sure that it is a spontaneous picture and not something you have contrived and generated yourself. Ask yourself or give your subconscious the command to tell you whether this image matches the target picture. Then wait a few moments and see if you feel a sense of inner conviction that it does.
9. Rouse yourself and either tape or write out a description of the imagery you saw. It would also be helpful to draw any pictures that came to mind.
10. Now repeat this procedure with another one of the targets until you have focused on all six.

In order to determine whether or not you have actually picked up any information from the target, you may want to open the envelope and provide yourself with immediate feedback. This is understandable, and can give you some very basic idea of how well you are doing, especially at first. If you wish to objectively determine if you are learning to use your ESP, however, it is important *not* to open any envelope until you have psychically probed all six of them. Since each picture should be as different as possible from the others, you can feasibly stack the deck in your

*This technique is based on the visualization strategies Rhea White found commonly used by psychics. Please refer back to the introductory chapter for more details.

favor by opening one by one. This may give you the spurious idea that you are displaying ESP when you really aren't. For instance, if the first picture you use depicts a boy by a lake, you already know that probably none of the other pictures include a human figure or a body of water. By a process of elimination you might eventually discern what is likely to appear on some of the later targets. This type of bias would be very minor, but it is one you should take pains to avoid.

The best way to objectively score your sessions is to test yourself using all six of the target pictures before looking at any of them. Then ask a friend to number the envelopes for you, keep a record for himself of which targets came from which envelopes, and then shuffle them up and give them back to you. You should then take each target and read over all six of your transcripts and try to guess which *one* was actually designated for that specific picture. Go through this procedure six times, trying to match each target to one of the transcripts. If you can do this fairly reliably (say fifty percent of the time), this is pretty good evidence that you are developing ESP. It is important, however, that your friend not stay with you while you are trying to make the matchups. He might unintentionally cue you with his eye movements, facial expressions, or other subtle forms of communication. He should only consult with you after you have made your matchings.

The Free Association Technique

This is a less focused procedure, but it can be very valuable as you try to induce ESP-mediated imagery. It will also help you to learn how to discriminate between psychic images and neutral ones generated by your mind. You will need a tape recorder in order to implement this procedure properly:

1. Once again begin by relaxing and closing your eyes.
2. Give yourself the suggestion that you wish to clairvoyantly view the target on which you are focusing.
3. Switch on the tape recorder.
4. Now verbally describe all the mental imagery that floats before your eyes. Do not try to willfully generate this imagery or inhibit it. Just let it flow. Proceed for about half an hour.
5. Rouse yourself and reveiw the tape you have just made.
6. Specifically note any images that were unusual, persistent, especially vivid, or that had any noteworthy emotional tones.

7. Consolidate your images into a composite of what you think the target might be and write it out or draw it.

After you have followed a similar procedure for all the targets, you can judge the material by following the guidelines suggested for the mental command technique. You may wish to make a list of four or five related images that you think pertain to the target. This will make the judging process a little more time consuming and difficult, but will not materially alter it.

Inducing a Ganzfeld Setting

This is a more formalized procedure that draws on the same strategy you used for the free association technique. It uses a highly structured ritual or formula which some people find very conducive to enhancing or detecting their ESP potentials. It is also likely to induce a mildly altered state of consciousness, which in itself may be very conducive to ESP. This technique is a bit more complex than the other two described above, and you will need some equipment to implement it properly. You will require a lamp with a red light bulb, a ping-pong ball cut in half, some tape, cotton, a headset, a cassette player, and a tape recorder. You will also have to prepare a tape that will instruct you in the use of the ganzfeld setting. Since the ganzfeld works especially well for testing yourself for telepathy, it might also be best to conduct your ganzfeld settings along with a friend who will act as your agent.

To establish a formal ganzfeld setting for your ESP test, follow these procedures carefully:

1. Sit in a reclining chair in front of the red light. The light should be at eye level, no matter what position you assume.
2. Place your cassette player with the instruction tape next to you on the floor or on a nearby table along with the tape recorder.
3. Place the headset from the cassette over your ears.
4. Place the halved ping-pong balls over your eyes, tape them on, and place cotton into any cracks where light is leaking in.
5. Stare into the red light. Try to position the light and yourself so that the red field at which you are staring is totally diffused.
6. Click on the cassette with the prepared instructions, giving you directions for watching your imagery and attending to the target picture. Your tape should include the following directions: "In this experiment we want you to think out loud. Report all of the images, thoughts, and feelings which pass through

your mind. Do not cling to any of them. Just observe them as they go by. At some point during the session we will send you a message. Do not try to anticipate or conjure up this message. Just give yourself a suggestion—right now—that the message will appear in consciousness at the appropriate time. [Pause]

"Keep your eyes open as much as possible throughout the session and allow your consciousness to flow through the white noise which you will hear through the headphones.

"Release all conscious hold of your body and allow it to relax completely. As soon as you begin observing your mental processes, start thinking out loud. Continue to share your images, thoughts, and feelings verbally throughout the session."

7. After the message is over, allow the empty tape to continue playing. This will produce your white noise back ground and will constitute your auditory ganzfeld. Turn on your tape recorder.

8. Follow the directions on the tape by verbalizing all your thoughts, images, and feelings until the tape runs out or a timer you have set for half an hour goes off.

9. Rouse yourself and review the tape.

10. Notice any imagery that is persistent, especially vivid, or emotionally toned.

While you are undergoing the ganzfeld, you should have your friend or relative go to another room with a set of four to six magazine pictures or art prints. Each should be placed in a separate envelope. He should shuffle these and then randomly choose one and look at it for several minutes at some point during the session. He should consciously attempt to "send" the picture to you as he views it. His next job will be to place it back in its envelope, shuffle all the envelopes together, and hand the packages to you when you are finished with your session. You should then review all of the pictures and try to pick out the one that was actually sent to you. You should carry out this judging procedure without any help from your friend, who shouldn't even be with you in the room at the time you are making your decision.

In conclusion, remember that you are trying to learn or develop ESP. Don't expect instant success. Give yourself a chance to learn by your failures or mistakes. I took part in several ganzfeld sessions before I began noticing that I was beginning to tune in on the pictures sent to me.

References

Braud, W. G., Wood, R., and Braud, L. W. Free-response GESP performance during an experimental hypnagogic state induced by visual and acoustic ganzfeld techniques: a replication and extension. *Journal of the American Society for Psychical Research,* 1975, *69,* 105–14.

Charlesworth, Edward. Psi and the imaginary dream. In *Research in Parapsychology-1974.* Metuchen, New Jersey: Scarecrow Press, 1975.

George, Leonard. *Imagery Enhancement Training Program.* Handbook available from the author, 1982.

George, Leonard. Enhancement of psi functioning through mental imagery training. *Journal of Parapsychology,* 1982, *46,* 111–26.

Honorton, Charles and Harper, Sharon. Psi-mediated imagery and ideation in an experimental procedure for regulating perceptual input. *Journal of the American Society for Psychical Research,* 1974, *68,* 156–68.

Irwin, Harvey. Coding preference and the form of spontaneous extrasensory experiences. *Journal of Parapsychology,* 1979, *45,* 205–22.

Paivio, A. *Imagery and Verbal Processes.* New York: Holt, Rinehart & Winston, 1971.

Sargent, Carl. *Exploring Psi in the Ganzfeld.* New York: Parapsychology Foundation, 1981.

the role
of relaxation

Herbert Benson's *The Relaxation Response* hit the best-seller list in 1975. Soon manuals on TM (transcendental meditation), stress reduction, and anxiety-free living were selling like crazy. Similar books are selling this way even now. The general public is apparently willing to pay millions of dollars just to learn how to relax. Relaxation is becoming a goal sought after by millions of Americans tensed by all the hustle and bustle of everyday living.

What's so novel about relaxation? You might think that anyone could just sit back, lounge around, and sip a cool drink. But relaxation is, in fact, a much more complex mental and physical state. Over the last few years, doctors and psychologists have learned that physical relaxation is accompanied by several beneficial side effects. It has been found to decrease oxygen consumption, helps avert headaches and other physical complaints, and enables us to cope with the stresses of our jobs and home environments. Different techniques have been developed over the years to help the individual achieve a relatively relaxed and tension-free state. One of the oldest is called "progressive muscular relaxation." Using this rather cookbookish formula, the subject is taught to relax his body by progressively tensing and then releasing all the muscles systematically and gradually over the entire body. A newer approach is Herbert Benson's controversial meditative technique during which the subject merely sits in a comfortable position, relaxes all of his muscles, and then concentrates on his own rhythmic breathing.

Learning to relax is apparently not that difficult. But while doctors and mental health workers are studying the physical and psychological attributes of relaxation, a few parapsychologists are now discovering that relaxation may help all of us gain access to our ESP potentials as well.

The first contemporary parapsychologist to suggest that relaxation might be a key to uncovering our psychic abilities was Rhea White. I discussed in the introductory chapter how Ms. White made a detailed study of how psychics go about their work. She had long wondered why the great psychics of the past seemed to be so much better than gifted psychics tested in the laboratory today. Even J. B. Rhine had to admit, much to his chagrin, that during his early years at Duke University he had uncovered more gifted subjects than at any other time during his career. So Rhea began collecting accounts in which the star psychics of the past explained what they did, or what procedures they used to latch onto ESP impressions. She found that, by and large, many of the psychics began with relaxation.

One of the best-known psychics of yesteryear was Craig Sinclair, the wife of Upton Sinclair who recounted their ESP tests in his book *Mental Radio*. Mrs. Sinclair was remarkably successful at telepathically and clairvoyantly reproducing pictures drawn by her husband or friends. How did she do it? Relaxation was one key, she explained.

"By making the body insensitive I mean simply to relax completely your mental hold of, or awareness of, all bodily sensation," she wrote. " ... Drop your body, a dead weight, from your conscious mind ... To make the conscious mind a blank it is necessary to 'let go' of the body; just as to 'let go' of the body requires 'letting go' of the consciousness of the body. If, after you have practiced 'letting go' of the body, you find that your mind is not a blank, then you have not succeeded in getting your body rid of all tension. Work at it until you can let both mind and body relax completely."

Rhea White also found that the psychics she surveyed suggested quite a gamut of different relaxation techniques. Some proceeded to relax all of the muscles of the body progressively from the feet to the head, or vice versa. Others suggested that the student should lie down to relax, while others suggested that one should sit upright.

66

With overt clues such as these hidden away in parapsychology's historical literature, it was inevitable that parapsychologists would eventually begin to systematically investigate the relationship between ESP and physical relaxation. As I pointed out earlier, Ms. White's research was published in the *Journal* of the American Society for Psychical Research in 1964, but it wasn't until 1973, almost ten years later, that the results of the first hardline *experimental* work on ESP and relaxation was published in full.

The two parapsychologists who spearheaded the study of relaxation and ESP were the (then) husband and wife team of Drs. William G. and Lendell W. Braud. William Braud, a young, quiet, and introverted psychologist, was teaching at the University of Houston at the time. (He is now working at the San Antonio-based Mind Science Foundation.) Lendell Braud Williams contrasted sharply with her husband. Extroverted, lively, and effervescent, she now teaches at Texas Southern University.

For their first experiment, the Brauds used a single subject whom they described as "a twenty-seven-year-old male assistant professor of psychology at the University of Houston." As you might suspect, the subject was none other than William Braud himself, although this fact was camouflaged in the original report. For the experiment Dr. Braud sat in a comfortable armchair and closed his eyes. He was given instructions to systematically tense and then relax all the muscles of his body. When a state of muscular relaxation was achieved, Braud then relaxed mentally as well but kept in the back of his mind the suggestion that he would try to be open to any psychic impressions which came his way. Completely enveloped by this state of deep relaxation, Dr. Braud freely verbalized all the impressions and images which popped into his mind as he rested. These were, of course, tape-recorded. After the session was over, Dr. Braud also wrote out his impressions and sketched out the images he had perceived.

During this procedure an experimenter was stationed in a room on another floor of the building in which the test was run. This experimenter, who also acted as the telepathic agent for Dr. Braud, randomly selected a picture from 150 postcard-size targets. The pictures ranged from art reproductions to magazine collages and clippings. After the target had been selected, the agent tried to send its contents to Dr. Braud by concentrating on the shapes and colors accentuated in the picture, by tracing predominant shapes depicted on it, and even by imaging about anything directly associated with the target. All told, six sessions were run.

Dr. Braud turned out to be a rather striking subject. One of the targets depicted two Coke bottles with the caption, "It's the real thing. Coke," written beneath it. An additional picture of an antique car parked on a road was wedged between the bottles. After relaxing, Dr. Braud described the target in such detail that it is hard to figure out any explanation *except* ESP to account for it:

> " ... two crossed ... lines ... the 'X' appeared ... in the center upper left ... I vividly saw a glass, a frosted glass filled with Coca Cola. The glass appeared to be in the upper right hand area ... some secondary images ... a road in the center of the photo ..."

All six targets for the session were given to an independent judge along with the transcripts of Dr. Braud's psychic impressions for each of the tests. The judge was asked to determine which transcript matched which target and he was easily able to make a perfect match ... 6 out of 6.

Spurred on by their success, the Brauds expanded their relaxation research and tested additional subjects. Six students from the University of Houston were chosen, equally divided between the sexes. All six of the students underwent the same initial relaxation procedure as had Braud. The results were no less spectacular. Each subject volunteered for one session, so again there were 6 targets and 6 transcripts for the independent judge to match up. And once again he was able to make a perfect match. Some of the transcripts were startlingly accurate as well. When one target was a picture of a sleeping cow, the subject reported:

> " ... there appears one and then two structures which looked like the claws of a crab ... then they became horns with a cow's head attached ... a cow's head with horns on it ..."

Even more excited by their continuing success, the Brauds proceeded to test larger numbers of subjects. At first even these sizable groups did well on ESP tests given after relaxation instructions, but the Brauds' success soon faltered. They eventually discovered that larger groups of subjects did not seem to work out well. Three follow-up experiments were run, but all showed only chance results.

However, the Brauds were by no means through with their relaxation studies and designed two further tests to more accurately gauge how relaxation was really affecting their subjects' ESP. They were concerned that perhaps such complications as the subject's mood, expectancy, attitude, and other factors, and not the actual relaxation were mitigating their success.

In the first follow-up experiment, all of the subjects again underwent a progressive muscular relaxation exercise. But before they learned how well they had done on the ESP part of the test, the subjects rated their own degree of relaxation on a 10-point scale (one being extremely relaxed and ten being very tense). The Brauds then separated those subjects who had done well on the test and those who had not. They discovered that the successful subjects had given themselves a mean relaxation rating of 1.81 while the unsuccessful subjects gave an average rating of 3.12. So it would appear that the good ESP subjects at least subjectively felt that they were more relaxed than the poorer ones.

In order to be even more certain that it was the relaxation and nothing else that was promoting their success, the Brauds carried out one further experiment. However, in this group of tests the two psychologists did not rely upon self-rated scales. Instead, electromyographic recordings were taken from the frontalis muscle group (these are the muscles of the forehead) of each subject. This would tell the experimenters precisely how relaxed the volunteer was. Furthermore, before the ESP test was administered one group of subjects was given muscle-tensing instructions, while the other group received the relaxation exercises. As in the earlier experiments, after this conditioning the subjects tried to image about telepathically sent targets.

The results of this neat and trim experiment were just as you might have guessed. The relaxation group scored above chance, the tension group just at chance. The EMG recordings also proved that the relaxation group was more physically relaxed than the tension group. The Brauds also made the subjects fill out a lengthy questionnaire about their mood, attitude, expectancy, etc., towards and during the test. They found no correlation between these scales and the ESP scoring.

On the basis of these results the Brauds felt that they had aptly demonstrated a relationship between ESP and relaxation. This is hard to deny since Dr. Rex Stanford of St. John's University in New York has now replicated some of the Brauds' work. In discussing their findings, William and Lendell Braud have concluded succinctly:

"Subjects without any prior history of striking psychic experiences are shown to demonstrate reliable psi abilities while in a state of physical and mental relaxation."

This is a strong statement in itself, but the Brauds' conclusion raises more questions than it answers. Why should relaxation help a subject gain access to his ESP potentials? This is a question of growing importance. The Brauds suggest that in order to perform any task, a certain amount of "arousal" is needed. As the task becomes more difficult, the level of arousal needed to perform it decreases. In other words, arousal impedes or disrupts us from performing difficult tasks. ESP is certainly an unpracticed and difficult mental process, so low arousal and activation may help us develop it. Arguing from a different angle, the Brauds also suggest that we need a high degree of arousal in order to function in the world through the use of our sense perceptions. By attenuating our normal arousal level, ESP might be enabled to enter consciousness. Also, the Brauds continue, such a state might be beneficial to our survival. As we cut outselves off from gaining sensory information about the outside world, we might use ESP as a substitute information channel to monitor our environment.

Although the Brauds have had little success when testing large groups with relaxation conditioning, three young researchers from the former Maimonides Medical Center's division of parapsychology and psychophysics have had better luck using an ingenious variant of the relaxation technqiue. They have used this approach in testing large audiences attending public information lectures they have given on ESP. Ellen Messer, Pat Barker, and Sally Drucker would first give the audience a presentation on parapsychology which included a film of a successful ESP test taken live at the division. Afterward, the group was invited to try their hand at an ESP test themselves. First though, Ms. Messer conducted the audience in a group relaxation procedure using progressive muscular relaxation. This exercise lasted from ten to twenty minutes. After this initial relaxation period, the audience would be asked to keep their eyes closed and to keep track and take note of all mental images which came to mind. At this time one of the experimenters would go into another room and select a target picture from a pool of over 1000. She would then try to send it to the audience telepathically. In order to guess at the target each participant would fill out a scoring sheet. Each member guessed which of ten categories were included or not included in the target picture; was it in color or black and white, did it depict motion, did it show people, body parts, artifacts, architectural features, animals, food, or mythical figures? So each person made ten guesses declaring whether each of these categories was present or absent.

The results were interesting to say the least. No one ever got nine or ten correct guesses individually. And subjects who jotted down their visual impressions on the back of the forms rarely described anything similar to the target. But the experimenters also took a group score, asking for a show of hands from the audience in order to take a majority vote on which categories were included in the target. (A man holding a cat, for instance, would be scored as having animal and human figures but not other categories unless it were in color.) Misses Messer, Barker, and Drucker observed that the group *as a whole* had often seemed to perceive the target and would correctly guess by majority vote sometimes nine out of ten categories for a specific target even though no *one* person was very accurate. Apparently as the group relaxed, the ESP information was somehow diffused throughout the entire audience.

Of course, systematic relaxation is not the only technique one can use to relax. Ever since biofeedback became all the rage in the 1970s, there has been quite a bit of speculation within some parapsychological circles that ESP might be relatd to certain brain waves that are indicative of mental and physical quietude. This idea held out the promise that, through the control of such brain waves, one might learn to be psychic. Special emphasis was placed on the possible role of the alpha rhythm, which commonly occurs when a person is in a relaxed state of mind and body. These appear on the EEG as waves ranging between 8–13hz.

This idea received some impetus in 1969 when Charles Honorton at the Maimonides Medical Center reported the results of an experiment that seemed to link ESP with alpha brain waves. Honorton had recruited ten high school students who were asked to guess the symbols on standard ESP cards while their brain waves were monitored. His findings indicated that the subjects did best when they were indeed producing alpha waves. The only problem with the experiment was that all the students had scored above chance on some earlier card-guessing tests and were therefore gifted ESP subjects to begin with. So the tests didn't suggest that ESP could necessarily be "learned" through biofeedback or alpha brain wave production.

Interest in the brain's electrical rhythms nonetheless spurred on quite a bit of subsequent research on ESP and the alpha rhythm, but the results were often confusing and contradictory. Some researchers found a negative correlation between ESP and alpha generation, while others found no relationship at all. Research was published showing that gifted meditators and psychics could perform especially well while producing alpha, yet replication of this research was nil in coming. Then there were studies showing that increased production of alpha was related to vari-ability in the subject's ESP scores, or that increase in the *frequency* of the alpha rhythm was related to scores on ESP card-calling tests. The bottom line was that there didn't seem to be any simple relationship between alpha waves and ESP, and soon research exploring any possible connec-tion was abandoned.

Researchers who have been studying the nature of biofeedback and brain waves have also been fascinated by theta waves. These are slower waves than alpha and only occur when the brain and body are very quiet. They show up in the EEG tracings taken of meditators, people deeply involved in creative imagery, and during reverie. Theta waves are much more difficult for most people to control than the commoner alpha waves, yet some ability to generate them can be learned through biofeedback. There is also some impressive anecdotal evidence that the state of mind typified by the production of theta waves may be conducive to the emergence of ESP.

This curious finding was made by Dr. Elmer and Alyce Green, who pioneered the scientific study of biofeedback in the 1960s and 70s at the Menninger Foundation in Topeka, Kansas. Part of their original research was devoted to training their subjects in the production of theta waves. The volunteers who participated in the pilot studies invariably spoke of entering into a deeply relaxed, near-sleep state in which they found themselves immersed in a world of mental imagery. Several times as they were training their subjects, the Greens ran into incidents that smacked of genuine ESP. They most commonly noted these incidents when their subjects were sealed in an experimental room where they were being taught to control the theta wave. The subjects were asked to verbally report any imagery they might experience, and some of these mental pictures seemed to reflect what was occurring elsewhere in the building.

The first time this happened was when a young woman was being trained. "While she was lying on the couch in the experimental room (fifteen feet from the control room and separated from it by a hallway)," Green reported, "a research assistant came to the control room and said I was wanted upstairs for a long-distance telephone call. I left the lab (in the basement of the research building) and went upstairs to my office on the other side of the building. There I found that Swami Rama (a well-known Indian yogi) was calling about a research plan.

"When I returned to the control room a few minutes later, I heard the subject saying that she had thought of Swami Rama and suddenly had an image of him in the experimental room. He did not say anything, just smiled and stood there for a couple of minutes, and then disappeared."[*]

A similar incident occurred when one of the Greens' associates was learning to generate theta waves.

[*]From *Beyond Biofeedback* ©1977 by Elmer Green and Alyce Green. Reprinted by permission of Delacorte Press/Seymour Lawrence.

"In the middle of the session," continues Green, "a loud crash and thump from the floor above sent me upstairs to ask for quiet during the experiment. When I reached the first floor I found that three workmen had just brought in some large plants in heavy pots for an interior garden they were constructing in the building. One of the plants was intended for a trellis, but at the moment its bright green leaves and several branches were lying across and trailing over a low fieldstone wall. I told the workers that we were running an experiment, and they said they were through for the day anyway.

"When I returned to the lab, Alyce asked me what had caused the thump. When I told her about the plants, both she and our research assistant laughed. Dale had just said, before I entered the room, that he had the image of a plant, and suddenly he *was* the plant, 'a very green plant,' that was lying on or fallen over a low rock wall."

Nor was Green himself immune to these flashes of ESP. During one of his own sessions, he kept seeing images of his research assistant continuously arranging and rearranging blocks of colored paper. Green thought the images somehow related to time and his assistant's attempts to fit a number of events into a specific time sequence. Only after the session was over was Green to learn the truth of his intuition. While he was practicing in the laboratory room, his assistant (who was monitoring the experiments) was mentally trying to figure out how she was going to rearrange all the plans for her wedding. Her fiancé's military commitments had necessitated the rescheduling.

Alyce Green also witnessed a few psychic experiences while participating in the theta project. She also reported in her contribution to *Beyond Biofeedback* how one of her subjects had a vivid precognitive experience while learning to control his theta waves. During his session he heard a voice telling him that he had been accepted to a graduate school in Wichita, which seemed to predict the exact message his college roommate gave him back at his apartment later that day. The student later complained to the Greens that the incident seemed to open up his psychic senses. He had several more precognitive experiences spontaneously during the week and eventually became spooked by the whole thing. He grew even more uncomfortable when he dreamt of the George Wallace assassination attempt just the day before it happened. Counseling with the Greens relieved his anxiety.

To date, though, no research specifically studying the relationship between ESP and theta waves has been reported. So these anecdotes can only be considered suggestive. It is interesting to note, however, that theta waves are linked to meditation which is an art that also stresses relaxation. And one of the ultimate goals of some forms of meditation, including TM, just happens to be the development of psychic abilities.

Through the popularization of Transcendental Meditation, the practice of meditation is now flourishing among businessmen, housewives, and academicians alike in the United States. Promising both physical and psychological benefits, TM offers a simple yet ritualistic means of relaxation. Dr. Herbert Benson, now an associate professor of medicine at Harvard Medical School, was so enthralled by the results of his own tests which gauged the psychophysiological benefits of TM that he wrote in the *Harvard Business Review* that " ... transcendental meditation (TM) results in physical changes that are consistent with generalized decreased sympathetic nervous system activity and are thus opposite to the fight-or-flight response." In other words, the practitioners were relaxed!

Benson himself, though, became disenchanted with TM's ritual initiations and procedures and soon developed his own relaxation technique which was summarized at the beginning of this chapter. This has excited no simple controversy between supporters of Benson and the TM-ers, each group claiming that it has the better technique.

Although there have been no official reports on whether TM helps a person unlock his ESP potential, it is widely believed that yogic disciplines will gradually help an individual unfold psychically. There is, however, a widespread, though erroneous, belief in the West that the principal yogic doctrines (namely the *Yogic Aphorisms of Patanjali*) warn the student to be wary of psychic gifts (or Siddhis). This is Aphorism #37. However, even this warning only relates to *certain* psychic powers and is not a blanket condemnation of seeking to develop psi capabilities *per se*. The late Arthur Koestler has aptly pointed out this fact in his book, *The Lotus and the Robot*:

> " ... This aphorism is the *only* warning in the entire text; and it only refers to certain psychic powers mentioned in the preceding paragraphs, whereas the powers which are listed after the warning, such as entering into another's body, omnipotence and levitation are held out as legitimate rewards to those who master the higher forms of contemplation. As for the later sources, the *Hatha Yoga Pradipika* and its companion texts, the eight siddhis are promised on practically every page in renumeration for more difficult mudras."

There has not been a great deal of ESP research carried out on the relationship between yoga, meditation, and relaxation. But a first step has been taken by Dr. Gertrude Schmeidler, the well-known parapsychologist who teaches psychology at the City College of the City University of New York. Dr. Schmeidler asked a Swami to instruct a class of a few students in a simple yogic breathing exercise (similar, in fact, to the procedure which Benson has developed to aid relaxation). She also tested the students with ESP cards before and after the session. After the exercises, Dr. Schmeidler found that all her students' scores went up! Was this due to relaxation? Did the students perform better because they expected to? Did the Swami have some sort of psychic influence over them?

Unfortunately, very little research has been designed to determine if meditation practices are linked to ESP. This is an area where considerable research is still needed and may be a fruitful line of inquiry.

In conclusion, it certainly looks as though relaxation in itself may be a royal road to ESP. Future research will now have to focus on what form of relaxation will best do the trick, or what mental disciplines will augment the psi-conducive nature of physical relaxation.

LEARNING TO RELAX

Learning to relax is a little more complex than you might think. It is a skill that you must learn to master, just as you would any other talent. The total relaxation of the mind and body entails more than just sitting back and daydreaming. Our lives are so filled with stress, tension, anxiety, and mental preoccupations that true relaxation is as hard to attain as the legendary *samadhi* of yoga. Learning to relax is not something to be taken lightly, which is why entire books have been written about relaxation and stress reduction. Please remember that we today are the result of our ancient heredity; the result of times past when we lived in the wilds and had to compete with other animals and outrun potential predators in order to survive. You might say that relaxation just isn't in our genes. The human nervous system is structured for vigilance so that we will be ready to fight or flee at a moment's provocation. So if you wish to learn the gentle art of relaxation, it is going to take as much time and commitment as it does to master visualization, dream control, or any other mind game.

The most common form of relaxation is progressive muscular relaxation, a procedure that teaches you how to relax the body by working with each of the body's muscle groups in succession. The goal of the system is to train yourself to recognize the difference between a state of muscle tension and relaxation. This way you will gradually learn to recognize when you are really relaxed. Before beginning to practice this system as outlined below, however, keep several factors in mind. Always practice progressive muscular relaxation at a place and time when it is unlikely that you will be disturbed. (This of course goes for any relaxation procedure.) You can practice in a reclining chair, couch, or bed, though you might find that a bed works best initially. As you begin the procedure by alternately tensing and relaxing your muscles, don't tense them to the point where they feel cramped. Just tense the muscles until they feel taut. The next important thing to remember is not to let your mind wander. Concentrate on what you are doing by keeping your full attention on that area of the body with which you are working. Learning to relax is a mental as well as physical exercise. For this reason you might try identifying yourself with the area of the body you are exercising. You might even go so far as to project your consciousness to the part of the body being relaxed. Merge totally with each part of your own body. This exercise will help reduce messages arising from other parts of the body that might distract you. To put it bluntly, you can't very well relax your leg when your nose is itching and driving you crazy!

You might also want to couple your tension and release phases with breathing techniques. It is sometimes helpful to inhale as you tense a muscle group and exhale gradually as you release it. But let your breathing come naturally. Don't force or overdo it, or you will find yourself focusing more on your breathing than on your body. That's fine for yoga but not for progressive muscular relaxation. Closing your eyes might also help you focus more completely on your exercises.

Read over these suggestions several times before you actually begin practicing. When you have digested them, you can begin to put what you know into practice.

The following is a brief course in how to go about progressively relaxing the muscles of the body. Note how each specific muscle group is covered in the procedure. You might find it more expedient to slightly alter the sequence of the muscle groups, but this is something you will have to find out for yourself. Such minor deviations shouldn't materially interfere with your goal of total relaxation.

1. Take a series of deep breaths. Breathe in slowly, hold for about five seconds, and then release just as slowly.
2. Begin by clenching your dominant fist, hold it, and count to five, release and repeat two or three times.

3. Repeat the procedure by flexing the dominant bicep.
4. Repeat with the nondominant fist.
5. Repeat with the nondominant bicep.
6. Take a short break and concentrate on the feeling of relaxation and inner warmth, or the satisfaction that the feeling of relief gives you.
7. Repeat with the muscles of the forehead by either raising or furrowing your eyebrows.
8. Repeat by closing and opening your eyes, if you are working with your eyes open.
9. Repeat by clenching your jaw.
10. Take a short break as described in 6.
11. Tense and release the neck muscles by either working with the muscles or, if you have a hard time feeling this group, by touching your chin to your chest.
12. Tense and relax the shoulder blades by arching them backward.
13. Repeat by pushing your shoulders forward.
14. Tighten and then relax the stomach.
15. Repeat with the sphincter (rectal) muscle.
16. Repeat with the thighs.
17. Tense and relax the toes by curling them as tightly as you can.
18. Repeat by pulling your toes toward your body.
19. Tense and relax your dominant leg muscle.
20. Repeat with the nondominant leg muscle.
21. Stop and try not to move. Focus your mind on your state of total relaxation and enjoy it.

How will you know when you have achieved a state of total relaxation? When you have reached this state, you may find that you feel as though you are existing without any body at all. This won't frighten you or bother you since you'll simply be too relaxed to get uptight about anything. (This is why progressive muscular relaxation is sometimes used in psychotherapy to help a patient overcome a phobia. The patient is taught to visualize the object of his fear while so relaxed that he cannot respond with fear or anxiety. This breaks the vicious circle that constantly reinforces the phobia, and the patient unlearns the irrational response.) I personally can tell when I have achieved total relaxation by what I call the "inertia" response. This is a state where I am so comfortable that the very idea of moving so much as a hand or foot bothers me. I feel as though I would have to make a momentous effort to even flinch.

The fact remains, though, that some people don't learn well by themselves. These individuals do better if taught how to relax by a guide.

The best way to proceed is with the use of a tape recording. Commercially available tapes instructing you in the art of relaxation are sold by many self-help organizations and bookstores, but you can do just as well as preparing one yourself. Printed below is the text that the Brauds used during the ESP tests that were described in the first part of the chapter. It was adapted from a standard procedure used in general psychology. If you are a man, it helps if a female reads the instructions. The alternate is true if you are a woman. The speaker should intone the instructions in a soft and almost monotonous voice, as though he or she were trying to hypnotize as well as relax you. For an even better effect, some sort of quieting background noise—such as the sounds of ocean waves—might heighten the results:

The purpose of this tape is to induce a state of physical and mental relaxation. We will begin with muscular relaxation. Relaxation is the elimination of all muscular tension. Get as comfortable as you can; loosen any clothing that may be too tight. When you relax, do not think about the instructions. Just follow them passively and automatically. When tensing any part of your body, remember to leave all other muscles completely relaxed. Begin by curling your toes downward into a tense position. Tense up more and more and notice the discomfort. Hold this tension while I count from ten to one, letting go at the count of one. (Count) Relax. Now relax your toes completely, and feel the difference. Instead of curling your toes, arch them up toward your face and feel the tension and discomfort all along your shins. Hold this ... (Count from ten to one) ... relax. Feel the relief in your legs. Next, curl your toes again and tense up your entire legs and calves, making sure the rest of your body is completely relaxed ... (Count) ... relax. Enjoy the feeling of relief that accompanies the removal of muscular tension. Relax all tension, release all pressures, place your body in a state of deep relaxation, going deeper and deeper every time. Next, tense your stomach muscles as tighly as you can as I count ... (Count) ... relax. Let go completely. Relax. Arch your back now, and feel the tension all along your spine ... (Count) ... relax. Settle down comfortably again. Let go of all of your weight; let go of all of the tension in every muscle of your body. Now focus your attention on your arms and fists. Relax the rest of your body completely. Tense your fists and bend your arms at your elbows, flexing your biceps. Hold this as tightly as you can ... (Count) ... relax. Let your arms flop to your sides. Relax completely. Now, take in a deep breath, fill your lungs, feel the tension all over your chest. Hold it ... exhale. Feel the relief as you exhale. Relax. Make sure that all of the body parts that we have concentrated on are completely relaxed. If there is any tension, relax those muscles completely. Now press your head back as far as it will go. Feel the tension in the muscles of your neck ... (Count) ... relax. Bend your head forward now ... touch your chest with your chin ... (Count) ... relax. Remove all strain and tension. Relax your neck ... your throat ... mouth ... relax your scalp ... smooth out the muscles of your forehead ... relax your eyes, and all of your facial muscles. Relax ... relax ... relax. Relax every muscle of your body. Focus on that area which is most relaxed and imagine that same pleasant, positive relaxing feeling to spread, engulfing your entire body in one comfortable, warm, pleasant feeling of relaxation. Relax totally and completely.

We will now begin mental relaxation. Hold your head straight and lift your eyes upward in order to strain the eyes. Do not blink. Your eyelids will become heavy; your eyelids will become tired. While waiting for this effect, take a deep breath, and while exhaling, imagine yourself becoming more deeply relaxed. Imagine relaxing more and more with each breath. When your eyes feel heavy and tired, do not force them to remain open. Close your eyes when they become tired. Take deep breaths, and with each exhalation, become more deeply relaxed. Now, concentrate again on relaxing ... relaxing your whole body. Relax all tension ... release all pressures. Place your body in a state of deep relaxation, going deeper and deeper. Make certain that all muscles are completely relaxed. It feels so good to be completely and totally relaxed. Noises and sounds will not distract you, but will help you to become more mentally at ease and more relaxed.

It might be pertinent to point out that a debate has raged within conventional psychology over whether taped or directly spoken instructions work best. There is some evidence that greater relaxation is achieved when the instructions are directly spoken to the subject and not merely recited over a tape recorder. But such a procedure isn't too practical for home testing. Since you will be using these exercises as a learning aid, you should be able to master your own optimal state of muscular relaxation no matter which procedure you use.

Since working with progressive muscular relaxation, Dr. William Braud and Dr. Lendell Braud Williams have discovered that a multisystem approach to relaxation works even better for ESP training. They have developed a tape which not only relaxes the body, but helps reduce random "noise" from the mind and sense organs. This tape is geared toward helping the subject relax both the mind and the body, while making him or her potentially open to ESP impressions. The tape relies on progressive muscular relaxation, autogenic exercises, visualizations, and breathing instructions. It has been widely distributed and used by parapsychologists, and with some provocative results. The following is the text of the tape:

We'll begin with physical relaxation. Relaxation is the elimination of all muscular tension. Make yourself as comfortable as you can. When you relax, do not think about the instructions. Just follow them passively and automatically. When tensing any part of your body, leave all other muscles completely relaxed. Begin by curling your toes downward into a tense position. Tense up more and more and notice the discomfort. Hold this tension ... now let go ... relax. Relax your toes completely, and feel the difference. Instead of curling your toes, arch them up toward your face and feel the tension and discomfort all along your shins. Hold this tension ... relax. Feel the relief in your legs. Next, curl your toes again and tense up your entire legs and calves, making sure the rest of your body is completely relaxed. Hold this tension ... relax. Enjoy the feeling of relief that accompanies the removal of muscular tension. Relax all tension, release all pressures, place your body in a state of deep relaxation, going deeper and deeper every time. Now, tense your stomach muscles as tightly as you can. Hold this tension ... relax ... relax. Let go completely. Relax. Arch your back now, and feel the tension all along the spine. Hold this tension ... relax. Settle down comfortably again. Let go of all of your weight. Let go of all of the tension in every muscle of your body. Now focus attention on your arms and fists. Relax the rest of your body completely. Tense your fists and bend your arms at your elbows, flexing your biceps. Hold this as tightly as you can ... relax. Let your arms flop to your sides. Relax completely. Now, take in a deep breath, fill your lungs, feel the tension all over your chest. Hold this breath ... exhale. Feel the relief as you exhale. Relax. Make sure that all of the body parts that we have concentrated on are completely relaxed. If there is any tension relax those muscles competely. Now, press your head back as far as it will go. Feel the tension in the muscles of your neck. Hold that tension ... relax. Relax your neck. Relax your head. Bend your head forward now ... touch your chest with your chin. Hold that tension ... relax. Relax completely. Now, tightly squinch up all the muscles of your face and around your eyes, making a face. Hold this tension ... relax. Remove all strain and tension. Relax your neck ... your throat .. your mouth ... even relax your tongue ... relax your scalp ... smooth out the muscles of your forehead and your scalp ... relax your eyes, and all of your facial muscles. Relax ... relax. Relax every muscle of your body. Focus on that area which is most relaxed and imagine that same pleasant, positive, relaxing feeling to spread, engulfing your entire body in one comfortable, warm, pleasant feeling of relaxation. Relax totally and completely. Scan your body again for the slightest bit of muscular tension. If you find tension anywhere relax it. Relace it with relaxation ... until your entire body is limp and loose and relaxed, like an old rag doll would appear to be. And you are that relaxed. Your relaxation will continue and will deepen through the remainder of the tape. Now take a deep breath ... and exhale ... and as you exhale, you relax more and more. With each breath, you're becoming more deeply relaxed. To relax even more deeply, count with me mentally from ten to one and with each count, feel yourself going deeper and deeper into a profound relaxed state ... an ideal state. (Count from ten to one, slowly) Relax.

AUTOGENIC EXERCISES. Having relaxed your muscles to a very low and comfortable level, you'll now relax your autonomic nervous system. The intended effects will occur naturally and automatically as you repeat to yourself the phrases you're about to hear. Don't exert any effort whatsoever; don't try to make these changes occur. Just passively attend to the parts of your body as they are mentioned, and the effects will automatically occur. Don't try to make anything happen, because it will happen on its own as you mentally repeat these phrases:

I feel quite quiet. I am beginning to feel quite relaxed. My feet feel heavy and relaxed. My ankles, my knees, and my hips feel heavy, relaxed, and comfortable. My solar plexus, the whole central portion of my body, feels relaxed and quiet. My hands, my arms, and my shoulders feel heavy, relaxed, and comfortable. My neck, my jaw, and my forehead feel relaxed. They feel comfortable and smooth. My whole body feels quiet, heavy, comfortable, and relaxed. I feel quite relaxed.

My arms and hands are heavy and warm. I feel quite quiet. My whole body is relaxed and my hands are warm ... relaxed and warm. My hands are warm. Warmth is flowing into my hands. They are warm ... warm. All of my extremities are heavy. All of my extremities, especially my hands, are warm.

My heartbeat is calm and regular. My heartbeat is regular and calm. My entire circulatory system is functioning flawlessly, smoothly, regularly.

It breathes me. My breathing is calm and regular. My breathing is very peaceful and regular. It's taking care of itself. It's as though something is breathing me. In ... out. Calmly. Regularly.

My solar plexus, the central area of my body is warm.

My forehead is cool. My forehead and the area around my forehead is cool.

I am very peaceful, quiet, and relaxed. My extremities are heavy. My extremities, especially my hands, are warm. My heartbeat and respiration are calm and regular. My solar plexus, the central portion of my body, is warm. My forehead is cool.

This relaxed and quiet state will continue and will become even more profound as you listen to the rest of this tape.

81

CONCENTRATE UPON CANDLE IMAGE. Concentrate on the image of a candle. Pay attention only to that candle. Push gently from your mind all other thoughts, all other sensations. Focus your attention only on the candle—its color, its shape. Don't think about the candle. Don't think about what you might do with it or where it comes from or anything else. Just the candle itself. Let your mind dwell only on that candle until I ask you to stop. (Pause for two min.) Very good. Now stop imaging the candle. Forget all about it.

NATURAL ENVIRONMENT IMAGERY. Maintain your state of deep relaxation while you image the natural environment. Imagine the scenes you might see as vividly as you can, as you listen to these natural sounds.

ABSTRACT IMAGERY. Continue to relax. Continue to visualize novel forms before your eyes—abstract images moving across your visual field. See how easy it is to image in three dimensions. Visualize figures moving in depth ... enhanced depth ... vast expanses of three-dimensional space.

KINESTHETIC IMAGERY. Again, maintain your state of deep relaxation ... maintain your stillness ... as you imagine yourself gliding through space. Imagine you're now entering your imagery. You're flying, floating in three-dimensional space ... gracefully, effortlessly ... turning somersaults through space ... dancing ... gliding in the air. Imagine how it feels as you listen to this music.

CONCENTRATION UPON BREATHING. You've been exercising your mind. It's now time to relax it. You'll now still your mind. Concentrate again on your breathing. Put all other thoughts gently out of your mind, and focus your attention completely on your breathing. Nothing will disturb you. Your body is relaxed ... from the tip of your toes to the top of your forehead. Your internal systems are functioning flawlessly, peacefully, regularly, and calmly. Relax deeply. All of your muscles are still. Your mind now is still. Forget all the thoughts from before and let your mind be as still as a peaceful mountain lake. No thought ripples will disturb it. This mental stillness and quietude will increase as you focus on your breathing ... as your breathe in ... and out ... in ... and out. Nothing else matters but your breathing. Focus only on your breathing, especially the transition point between breathing in and breathing out. Focus your attention effortlessly on that transition or changing point between breathing in ... and breathing out. Continue to focus on your breathing until I ask you to stop.

INSTRUCTIONS FOR MENTAL STILLNESS AND QUIETUDE. Relax completely. Rid your mind of mundane problems, and make your mind blank. Still, quiet, and blank. Focus on a circle of blankness before your mind's eye. A circular fence to keep out thoughts that may try to come in, like stray sheep. When a thought strays in, you must be very patient ... like a shepherd ... and push the stray out. No matter how many times it strays back, gently push it out. Your mind will be stilled. The circle will be blank. Your mind will be completely quiet.

To add to the tape's effect, the Brauds use selected musical extracts as a backdrop to the verbal instructions. The music changes according to the specific suggestions being employed. On page 84 is their list of extracts, which will give you an idea of what you might wish to use on your own tape. If you think that this is all a little too elaborate, just take a look at the following findings:

Lendell and William Braud reported on a pilot and confirmatory experiment using this tape in 1977. They tested over a hundred subjects both at their home and later at Texas Southern University. Each subject listened to the tape in a specially prepared room and was then instructed to "dream" about a picture that was being selected from another room where another experimenter was stationed. The target was a randomly selected art print or picture. The subject was shown four pictures after the session was concluded and asked to rank them according to how similar each one was to his or her mental imagery or impressions. If the subject ranked the target picture first or second, this was considered a hit. Rankings of three or four were considered misses. A first-choice ranking was designated a direct hit. During the confirmatory experiment in which 100 subjects were tested, the Brauds recorded thirty-six direct hits. This result would only occur by chance four times if the test were run 1000 times! In other words, the results weren't due to lucky guessing. Some other factor was at work ... namely, ESP.

The qualitative results of the experiment were also impressive. Van Gogh's painting *Boates at les Saintes Maries* was used for one session, and the subject responded with, " ... a boat, like Van Gogh's boat picture ... picture of Jesus and Mary ... seagull in flight, flying over rocks ... wood ... water fallng over statues in rock." You can't get any more direct than that! And when a *National Geographic* photograph of a snake's head was sent by ESP, the subject used in another one of the sessions mentioned visions of snakes three times during one part of the sending period.

Exercise	Background	Timing
Progressive muscular relaxation (with alternate tension)	*Music for Zen Meditation* Tony Scott Verve V6-8634	11 min.
Autogenic phrases	*Music for Zen Meditation*	5 min.
Concentration upon candle image	*Environments Disc 8* *Country Stream* Atlantic SD 66008	3 min.
Natural environment imagery	*Inside II Water* Paul Horn Epic KE 31600	9 min.
	Environments Disc I *Ocean* Atlantic SD 66001	
	Sonic Seasonings Rain Walter Carlos Columbia KG 31234	
	Snowflakes are Dancing Tomita RCA ARL1-0488	
	Environments Disc 2 *Dawn* Atlantic SD 66002	
	Mozart: Flute Quartet in C Major K. 285b Samuel Baron Concert-disc CS-215	
	Environments Disc 3 *Dusk* Atlantic SD 66003	
	Environments Disc 8	
Abstract imagery (novel images, depth)	*Peace Three* Beaver & Krause	2 min.
	Nonesuch Guide to Electronic Music HC-73018	
Kinesthetic imagery	*Electronomusic: Reflections of a String* John Pfeiffer RCA VICS-1371	2 min.
Concentration upon breathing	*Music for Zen Meditation* *Country Stream*	2 min.
Instructions for mental stillness and quietude	*Music for Zen Meditation* *Country Stream*	5 min.
Suggestion for "dream" of target	*Music for Zen Meditation* *Country Stream*	1 min.
	Total time	40 min.

It sure looks as though the Brauds are on to *something* with their tape. This tape is not commercially available at the present time. But the above instructions will give you enough background or ideas for preparing your own as you attempt to develop ESP.

Before you actually try testing yourself for ESP, you should practice with the procedures of your choice for at least a week. Unlike dream control or visualization, however, relaxation is a rather nonspecific route to ESP. It doesn't rely on any specific ESP mechanism or mediating vehicles such as mental imagery. It seems to be rather an all-encompassing ESP-conducive state. Of course, it is well known that physical relaxation helps induce mental imagery; but you can have a little more leeway in your approach to self-testing than you have with dream recall, ganzfeld stimulation, or imagery generation should you decide on relaxation as your route to psychic development.

Progressive muscular relaxation is best used, however, as an adjunct to visualization strategies. They tend to go hand in hand, as the content of the Brauds psi-conducive tape would tend to indicate. To test yourself for ESP during a state of relaxation, it would probably be best to use the "mental command technique" or the "free association technique" that were outlined in the previous chapter. Use the identical method of target preparation and adjudication, and follow those procedures faithfully. There is no need to revise them. Another procedure you might use is to include specific instructions for developing and exhibiting ESP as part of your tape. Many people are influenced by mental suggestions, especially if they are offered firmly by an authority figure. This is one of the reasons why hypnosis works and why (as you will see in the next chapter) this curious state seems to be yet another royal road to ESP. Some parapsychologists even believe that the ganzfeld setting works because of the expectancy instilled in the subject when the instructions about observing your mental imagery are read. In fact, when I first began running ganzfeld sessions at the Maimonides Medical Center's parapsychology laboratory, one of the first things I was taught was *how* to read these instructions for maximum effect.

You might therefore wish to include specific suggestions for demonstrating ESP at the end of your relaxation tape, or at least add it on when you are finally ready to test yourself for ESP. The Brauds included just such a set of instructions at the end of their psi-conducive tape and you may wish to adopt something similar:

You'll continue to be more relaxed than you've ever been. And when I stop talking, and you hear a hissing sound, you're going to have something like a dream. A very vivid and realistic dream about the target in the envelope. You'll see it clearly ... very clearly. It'll be as though you're walking right into the picture ... observing it from that standpoint ... participating in it. You'll see it very clearly and it will be very interesting and enjoyable. Your dream will continue for about five minutes, and then you'll awaken, refreshed, and report the dream, that is, write your impressions on paper. Describe the dream, the dream about the target. You'll remember it in great detail. So now, relax your mind ... relax your body. When you hear the hissing sound begin, a dream will spontaneously pop into your head ... a dream about the target. The dream will continue until the hissing sound stops. (*Five minutes of white noise*)

If you wish to use a similar set of instructions on your own tape, end with about five minutes of blank lead, which will produce a very effective white noise for you.

You can also test yourself for ESP with the use of standard ESP cards, if you are a little wary or tired of mental imagery strategies. Commercially available decks consist of twenty-five cards, each printed with either a circle, cross, square, star, or wavy lines. In a "closed" deck, each symbol appears on exactly five of the cards. These decks are widely available at metaphysical book stores or from the Institute for Parapsychology in Durham, North Carolina. (See footnote page 87 for the address.)

If you decide to test yourself with ESP cards, your best bet is to begin with the DT (or "down through") method. Shuffle the cards completely, and I *do* mean completely, and then set them before you. Do this before you begin your relaxation session. After you have finished relaxing, call down through the pack in the order you feel they are stacked. You can either write out your responses or—so as not to disturb your level of relaxation—dictate them to a friend or into a tape recorder. You should make at least four runs each time you experiment, so you may wish to use four packs of pre-shuffled cards if you are working by yourself. You can check your responses against the order of the cards after you emerge from your relaxation. What you should *not* do is check the actual symbol printed on each card as you guess it. This will bias your responses since you will be able (consciously or unconsciously) to make educated guesses about the cards coming up at the bottom of the deck by keeping count of which symbols have already appeared. You might also begin to note (again even unconsciously) what tiny scratches or nicks on the backs of the cards are associated with the symbols appearing on the other sides. You might then think that you are demonstrating ESP when you start using the cards over and over, when in fact you are merely learning and responding to these sensory cues.

If you have a friend or relative who is willing to assist you, you can also test yourself for telepathy or what is called general extrasensory perception—i.e., a test situation in which either telepathy or clairvoyance is allowed to operate.

Have your friend sit in another room with the shuffled deck. He or she should then look at each of the cards individually and then signal you by voice or by a prearranged signal when you should make each guess. Tally your score at the end of the run.

I should note that there are two very different guessing strategies subjects tend to use while responding to ESP cards. Some subjects like to guess quickly with the first impressions that come to mind. Others like to take their time and wait for images of the actual symbols to pop up. There is no evidence that either of these strategies has any particular advantage, though many of the gifted subjects originally tested by J. B. Rhine and his associates at Duke University did tend to use a slow rate of response.

These are only the very basic procedures for testing yourself with ESP cards. Little more needs to be explained since this information is available in many other books and manuals.*

But how will you know when you are scoring above chance? The statistics used to evaluate card-guessing tests can be fairly complicated, but the following procedure is relatively straightforward and makes little demands on any statistical or mathematical expertise.

Since a deck of ESP cards consists of five each of five different symbols, an average or chance score is going to be five hits per run ... *more or less.* That's the catch. To properly determine if a subject is scoring better than chance, we have to know if his scoring is better than the *fluctuation* of any chance hitting that is bound to occur. We do this by comparing the observed deviation from chance per run (how many hits you made over and above the expected five) to the standard deviation— i.e., the margin of error we expect due to the fluctuation of chance. So to determine the results of your performance, simply divide the observed

---

*A manual for using card guessing and other simple procedures is available from the Institute for Parapsychology, College Station, Box 6847, Durham, North Carolina, 27706. The institute also sells ESP cards, recording sheets, and other materials. A price list is available on request. Refer also to *Parapsychology—frontier science of the mind* by J. B. Rhine and J. G. Pratt (Springfield, Ill.: Charles C. Thomas, 1957) for further and more detailed instructions.

deviation by the standard deviation. The resulting number is called the critical ratio. If you have carefully followed the above conditions for your experiment, any score above 2.3 suggests that ESP was operating. This converts to a probability value (or p. value) of approximately .02, which means that your results would only have occurred by chance twice in a hundred experiments.

Below is a table which gives you the standard deviations for various numbers of card runs. Next to it is a conversion chart for some of the more commonly encountered CRs.

Standard Deviation of Runs up to 20		Probability Values of Critical Ratios up to 4	
No. of runs	Standard Deviation	Critical Ratio	Probability
4	4.00	2.5	.012
5	4.47	2.6	.0093
8	5.66	2.7	.0069
10	6.32	2.8	.0051
15	7.75	2.9	.0037
16	8.00	3.00	.0027
20	8.94	4.00	.000063
25	10.00		
50	14.14		

If you happen to be somewhere where you don't have easy access to these charts, there is a shorthand way of calculating the standard deviation for a series of card-guessing runs. Merely take the square root of the number of runs you have completed and double it.

It is also advisable to determine how many runs you are going to do *before* you actually begin each session. That way you won't make the error of stopping after some initial success and before your scores begin regressing to mean chance expectation. This often happens by pure coincidence. The practice of "optional stopping" will cause your scores to be artifically inflated and look more impressive than they really are.

References

Barker, P.; Messer, E.; and Brucker S. A group majority vote procedure with receiver optimization. In *Research in Parapsychology-1975*. Metuchen: Scarecrow Press, 1976.

Beloff, John. ESP: the search for a physiological index. *Journal* of the Society for Psychical Research, 1974, *47*, 403–20.

Braud, L. W. and Braud W. G. Further studies of relaxation as a psi-conducive state. *Journal* of the American Society for Psychical Research, 1974, *68*, 229–45.

Braud, L. W. and Braud, W. G. Clairvoyance tests following exposure to a psi-conducive tape recording. *Journal* of Research on Psi Phenomena, 1977, *2*, 9–21.

Braud, W. G. and Braud, L. W. Preliminary explorations of psi-conducive state: Progressive muscular relaxation. *Journal* of the American Society for Psychical Research, 1973, *67*, 26–46.

Green, Elmer and Alyce. *Beyond Biofeedback*. New York: Delacorte Press, 1977.

Honorton, Charles. Relationship between EEG alpha activity and ESP in card-guessing performances. *Journal* of the American Society for Psychical Research, 1969, *63*, 365–74.

Koestler, Arthur. *The Lotus and the Robot*. New York: Harper & Row, 1960.

Schmeidler, Gertrude. High ESP scores after a Swami's brief instruction in meditation and breathing. *Journal* of the American Society for Psychical Research, 1970, *64*, 100–103.

Sinclair, Upton. *Mental Radio*. New York: Collier, 1964.

White, Rhea. A comparison of old and new methods of response to targets in ESP experiments. *Journal* of the American Society for Psychical Research, 1964, *53*, 21–56.

strategy **4**

the role
of suggestion

It should be obvious by now that the 1970s represented a tremendously important period in parapsychology's scientific evolution. Researchers engaged in the experimental study of ESP were becoming more and more convinced that telepathy, clairvoyance, and precognition were powers that everyone possessed or potentially possessed. It also finally looked as though we were uncovering methods by which these potentials could be unlocked. Everyone committed to finding correlations between ESP and internally focused states of consciousness was being rejuvenated with a new sense that parapsychology was about to make a breakthrough ... a breakthrough that would make ESP more reliable and perhaps more acceptable to the scientific community.

This gradual "democratization" of the sixth sense had relied on simpler and more simple techniques. Studying the way ESP manifested in dreams was an important and fruitful project, but it was also an extremely cumbersome one. Subjects had to spend whole nights in the lab, EEG technicians had to be recruited and trained, even the paper that recorded the subject's brainwaves (which indicated when he or she was dreaming) was expensive. The innovation of sensory isolation and simple relaxation techniques was a great boon for researchers. If nothing more, a pair of ping-pong balls and a red light bulb didn't cost very much, and the results obtained through these methods rivaled anything that had come out of the original Maimonides dream research.

I was actively involved in much of this activity since I worked at the Maimonides lab, which by this time constituted a whole division of parapsychology. In 1975 I must have conducted well over three dozen ganzfeld sessions alone. What so impressed me personally was how easy it was to implement and control our procedures. No one seemed to be too interested any more in some of the older and more elaborate states of consciousness that had been historically linked to ESP, such as dreaming, trance and—perhaps more importantly—hypnosis. These seemed too bothersome to explore now that new techniques for working with the sixth sense had been uncovered.

While all this fascinating research was being pursued in the United States, a talented young experimental psychologist at Cambridge Univeristy was conducting research on ESP as part of his doctoral work. He, too, had read about the new breakthroughs linking ESP to altered states of consciousness and decided to take up the challenge himself. He wanted to design an experiment, however, that truly demonstrated that it was the internal state itself—and not some other factor such as the subject's expectancies—that caused the critical successes we were seeing. So between October 1977 and March 1978, Carl Sargent (whose later research into the ganzfeld was summarized earlier in this book) conducted one of the most carefully thought out and thorough experiments into the relationship between ESP and inwardly focused states of attention ever undertaken. But Carl decided to focus not on the ganzfeld or simple muscular relaxation. He turned instead to an old tried-and-true method for helping people tap into their psychic potentials that had long fallen from grace in parapsychology—hypnosis and hypnotic suggestion.

Sargent began by recruiting forty subjects from among his friends and associates. The scene of the tests was the Psychological Laboratory at Cambridge University, located on picturesque Downing Street near the campus of Trinity College. All of the subjects believed in ESP, had participated in some of Carl's previous experiments, and were given a complicated personality assessment scale before the experiment actually took place. Each subject was then randomly placed in either the "hypnosis" group or in the "waking suggestion" control group. Carl realized that, in order to test whether hypnosis and not some other factor might be affecting the scoring, he had to test both groups under almost identical conditions. So the young psychologist took pains to equalize the testing procedures. Each of the subjects assigned to the hypnosis subgroup was escorted to a chair or couch, hypnotized, given suggestions to relax and focus internally, and was then asked to guess through two decks of ESP cards. The subject was simply told whether he was right or wrong after each trial. Subjects tested under the waking suggestion condition were treated similarly, although no hypnotic induction routine was read to them. These subjects were led to believe that they were participating in an experiment correlating ESP to personality factors. They had no idea that other subjects were being hypnotized as part of the project; so they were probably just as highly motivated to do well on the tests as were the hypnotized subjects. "The aim in doing this," Sargent later stated in his published report on the experiment, "was to provide some reasonably similar substitute for the hypnotic induction procedure." These subjects, too, were invited to relax, remain comfortable, and guess at the ESP cards.

The results of the experiment were almost exactly in keeping with what Carl expected ... or at least hoped to find. They firmly supported that the hypnosis itself, and not some confounding variable, had affected his subjects' ESP capabilities. Both groups scored significantly above chance, but the hypnosis group averaged close to 12 hits per run while the waking control group averaged about ten. The difference between these group scores is statistically significant. A study of the personality assessments contributed by both groups indicated that no psychological difference between them could account for the results.

Carl's own conclusion about the test was quite straightforward. He not only felt that he had answered many criticisms of the "altered states" approach, but that he had firmly demonstrated that hypnosis was a valid and effective tool for eliciting ESP from volunteer subjects. He was also enthusiastic about the implications of his results, and suggested in his report that "one advantage of hypnosis experiments over other psi-conducive states is the time/expense factor: hypnosis experiments, unlike dreams ... or ganzfeld ... experiments, require little equipment and are not so time-consuming. It is to be hoped that psi/hypnosis research, which has not been markedly popular in the last decades, will enjoy increased popularity in coming years."

These sentiments have been shared by other researchers as well. While working at the Maimonides Medical Center's dream laboratory nearly ten years earlier, Charles Honorton and Stanley Krippner had written "... it would appear that hypnosis provides one of the few presently available techniques for affecting the level of [ESP] test performance."

This was, of course, before the advent of the ganzfeld and other internal focusing procedures.

But just what is it about hypnosis that has excited the enthusiasm of so many researchers? Does it still remain a viable method for helping people develop psychic abilities? Can self-hypnosis be used to attain this same goal? These will be some of the issues we will be exploring in this chapter. But let's begin by tracing back through the history of hypnosis and its strange and capricious connection with the paranormal.

The early history of hypnosis was, in fact, directly linked with the study to psychic phenomena. The roots of what eventually became the study of modern hypnosis go back to 1766 when Franz Anton Mesmer, a medical student at the University of Vienna, proposed that a universal "fluid" exists in the universe. It was believed that this fluid linked man with his fellow man and even to all Nature as well. Mesmer later came to believe that he could regulate the movement of this substance within the human body by moving his hands or wands up and down a reclining subject. The practice of "animal magnetism" or "mesmerism" soon flourished when Mesmer went to Paris and demonstrated that he could cure diseases and disabilities through the procedure. He became the rage of France even though a royal commission sent to study his claims in 1784 ultimately denounced him. Mesmerism eventually lost much of its sensationalism and Mesmer retired to Switzerland to write his memoirs, in which he noted that some of his subjects became psychic during their trances and could read minds or foretell the future. He did not appear to become very intrigued or concerned about these unusual displays, however.

The study of mesmerism and its specific relationship to ESP was actually the project of the Baron de Puységur, a nobleman from Lyons who was one of Mesmer's leading disciples. He was a compassionate and intelligent man who was concerned with the wretched medical resources available to the poor living in the countryside. He felt that mesmerism might be a valuable treatment process that could be made readily available to them. De Puységur had an enlightened attitude about the practice of mesmerism and he eventually came to the conclusion that the secret of the art was actually the will of the practitioner, and not some sort of magical fluid flowing within the universe. During the years he was administering to the poor, he started to work with a peasant named Victor Race, who seems to have been an extraordinarily gifted mesmeric subject. Through his gifts de Puységur discovered the deep trance state of mesmerism, the nature of post-hypnotic suggestion, and what was later called the "higher phenomena" of mesmerism. De Puységur soon found that

Race could read minds, diagnose the ills of people brought to him, see into the future, and respond to mental commands while mesmerized. The nobleman later found other subjects gifted with all these talents.

Public displays of psychic phenomena soon became part and parcel of the mesmerist's repertoire and continued to delight audiences well into the 1800s. Soon similar phenomena were making their appearance in England as well as all over the continent. One scientist in Great Britain who was bitten by the mesmerism bug was Dr. John Elliotson, the inventor of the stethoscope and a physician at London's University College Hospital. He began practicing the art in the 1830s and by the 1860s was reporting that his entranced subjects could experience any tastes or smells to which he subjected himself. He also claimed that they would react if he pricked himself with a pin while remaining hidden from their sights. This phenomenon was dubbed the "community of sensations" and caused quite a stir within the ranks of Elliotson's professional colleagues. The medical fraternity was rather skeptical of anything concerning mesmerism at this time, and Elliotson soon found himself the focus of a number of bitter attacks. But even toward the end of his life, he never reneged on the validity of what he had witnessed.

Formal medical recognition of mesmerism didn't receive its first breakthrough, in fact, until 1847 when James Esdaile, a government physician working in India, demonstrated that surgery (and even amputations) could be successfully performed using mesmerism as the sole anesthesia. Further recognition came when James Braid, a surgeon from Scotland, suggested that mesmerism was actually a physiological state produced by certain types of induction procedures. This explanation took mesmerism, which was now renamed "hypnosis," out of the domains of occultism and into those of science and psychology. Despite the new credibility hypnotism achieved after it was so summarily rechristened, the practice soon fell from favor once again, but this time for a different reason. The discovery of chloroform reduced the value of hypnosis as an anesthetic. The "higher phenomena" of mesmerism also seemed to become gradually more elusive as the practice of hypnotism became more respectable. By the 1860s many mesmerists began complaining that they could no longer elicit clairvoyance, psychic diagnoses, and prophetic gifts from their subjects. So popular interest in mesmerism began to fade, and eventually became little more than a dark alley in psychology's plight to understand the unconscious. Not until relatively recently had it become truly popular within the mental health profession as a therapeutic tool.

Just why displays of the "higher phenomena" of mesmerism seemed to die out during the middle of the 19th century is a matter of considerable conjecture. It is one of the most fascinating historical puzzles which emerges from the rich history of mesmerism. Some contemporary authorities believe that the early reports that made so much of these wonders were probably unreliable. More than one scholar has suggested that many of the early mesmerists and their subjects faked the displays. This seems unlikely, although both factors probably played a small role in the sheer number of reports that emanated from these decades. A more logical explanation is that the strange world of mesmerism and animal magnetism probably attracted a great many people who were naturally psychic. Psychics tend to be good hypnotic subjects, so these individuals may well have become the very subjects the mesmerists used for their research and public displays. The mesmeric movement was overshadowed in the 1840s when the Spiritualist movement—which taught that communication with the dead was possible through psychics and mediums—burst on the scene. Table tilting and mediumship soon became national pastimes. The newspapers were soon swamped with stories covering the new movement. Many of the naturally gifted psychics who had previously been attracted to the mesmerists may simply have deserted them to take up the new challenge of Spiritualism ... which was more attractive, less occult, more popular, and much more lucrative!

It is also possible that displays of precognition and clairvoyance emerged from the mesmeric movement for purely social and cultural reasons. To the general public of the 18th and 19th centuries, mesmerism was a magical art. It seemed like a mystical and transpersonal state by which the mind could transcend the limits of the body, a quasi-religious practice attuning man to the higher forces of nature and the universe. Some people probably became highly psychic when mesmerized because they simply *expected* to display these powers. They saw them as natural outgrowths of the "magical ritual" to which they had been subjected. But mesmerism lost its mystical aura by the middle of the 19th century. By then it was becoming more and more obvious that hypnosis was a natural physiological and psychological phenomenon. The naturalization of mesmerism may well have destroyed the magical hold it had long exerted on the public, and people no longer expected to become psychic when under its magnetism.

This isn't to suggest that all attempts to link ESP with the hypnotic state necessarily failed after this naturalization process took place. Scattered reports about medical patients who became extraordinarily psychic after being hypnotized still came to light even until the turn of the century. Some of these reports are extremely impressive and simply can't be easily dismissed. The careful research of Dr. Pierre Janet, a psychiatrist from Le Hague, is typical in this respect. Janet issued a report in 1885 to the Société de Psychologie Physiologique in France concerning his discovery of one such gifted subject, whom he could hypnotize merely by exerting his silent will. He didn't have to utter a single word.

Leonie B. came to Janet's attention through the grace of his colleague Dr. Gibert, who was also a physician in Le Havre. She was a middle-aged peasant woman who had come to Dr. Gibert for medical treatment, and he soon discovered that she was an extremely gifted hypnotic subject. Janet explained to the Société how Leonie had become so attuned to Gibert's mind and will that he could place her in a deep somnambulistic state merely by willing it. She would also respond to his unspoken thoughts. If this weren't enough, Janet went on to explain that he himself had been called in on the case and had witnessed these wonders. His *pièce de résistance* was that he had personally learned the art of hypnotizing Leonie without her being aware of it. He could even hypnotize her from another room or building.

The report caused no little sensation, especially since Janet was an eminent psychiatrist. It also piqued the interest of several researchers, including some of the leading psychical researchers of the day. These included F. W. H. Myers and his brother, who had recently helped to organize the Society for Psychical Research in England in an attempt to place the study of psychic phenomena on a scientific footing. Also fascinated by the report was Dr. Julian Ochorowicz, a psychologist who was pioneering the study of ESP in Poland and France. So in April of 1886 a team of investigators arrived in Le Havre to experiment with Leonie and see if Gibert and Janet could reporduce their miracles under their supervision. They weren't disappointed. For a week they witnessed several successful demonstrations of Gibert's power of "suggestion at a distance," as they dubbed the phenomenon. The tests were usually carefully run so that no collusion could have taken place beforehand between Leonie and the hypnotists.

F. W. H. Myers eventually wrote a long report on his adventures, portions of which are worth reprinting. The following extract describes the first experiment he witnessed while Leonie was staying at the home of Dr. Gibert's sister. Myers and his colleagues were also visiting at Dr. Gibert's home at the time. The date was April 21:

97

At 5.50 p.m. (an hour which was selected by drawing lots among various suggested hours), Dr. Gibert retired to his study and endeavoured to send Madame B. to sleep in the Pavillon, at a distance of about two-thirds of a mile. She was to fall asleep in the *salon*; whereas she habitually sits in the *kitchen* of the Pavillon (a house occupied by Dr. Gibert's sister).

It was supposed that the command would take about 10 minutes to operate, and at about six Professor Janet, Dr. Ochorowicz, M. Marillier, my brother and myself entered the Pavillon, but found that Madame B. was not in the *salon* but in the kitchen. We immediately went out again, supposing that the experiment had failed. A few minutes later Professor Janet reentered with Dr. Ochorowicz, and found her asleep in the *salon*. In the somnambulistic state she told us that she had been in the *salon*, and nearly asleep when our arrival startled her, and had then rushed down to the kitchen to avoid us; had returned to the *salon* and fallen asleep as soon as we left the house. These movements were attested by the *bonne*, but it of course seemed probable that it was merely our arrival which had suggested to her that she was expected to fall asleep.

A more impressive demonstration followed the next day:

In the evening we all dined at M. Gibert's, and in the evening M. Gibert made another attempt to put her to sleep at a distance from his house in the Rue Sery—she being at the Pavillon, Rue de la Ferme—and to bring her to his house by an effort of will. At 8.55 he retired to his study; and MM. Ochorowicz, Marillier, Janet and A. T. Myers went to the Pavillon, and waited outside in the street, out of sight of the house. At 9.22 Dr. Myers observed Madame B. coming half-way out of the garden-gate, and was plainly in the somnambulistic state, and was wandering about and muttering. At 9.25 she came out (with eyes persistently closed, so far as could be seen), walked quickly past MM. Janet and Marillier, without noticing them, and made for M. Gibert's house, though not by the usual or shortest route. (It appeared afterwards that the *bonne* had seen her go into the *salon* at 8.45, and issue thence asleep at 9.15; had not looked in between those times.) She avoided lampposts, vehicles, etc., but crossed and recrossed the street repeatedly. No one went in front of her or spoke to her. After eight or ten minutes she grew much more uncertain in gait, and paused as though she would fall. Dr. Myers noted the moment in the Rue Faure; it was 9.35. At about 9.40 she grew bolder, and at 9.45 reached the street in front of M. Gibert's house. There she met him, but did not notice him, and walked into his house, where she rushed hurriedly from room to room on the ground-floor. M. Gibert had to take her hand before she recognized him. She then grew calm.

M. Gibert said that from 8.55 to 9.20 he thought intently about her; from 9.20 to 9.35 he thought more feebly; at 9.35 he gave the experiment up, and began to play billiards; but in a few minutes began to will her again. It appeared that his visit to the billiard-room had coincided with her hesitation and stumbling in the street. But this coincidence may of course have been accidental.

Myers and his colleagues supervised a total of twenty-five attempts on the part of Dr. Gibert to hypnotize Leonie from a distance. They were able to chalk up nineteen successes.

The most fascinating aspect of Janet's research, however, was the probable role that learning may have played in Leonie's psychic development. Dr. Gibert had introduced her to hypnosis as part of her medical treatment. While it is certainly possible that she had always been psychic, it is also possible that—through her repeated exposure to the hypnotic state—Leonie eventually became so sensitive to Gibert's will that his influence over her carried into her waking hours. It seems odd that this possibility was not apparent to the psychical researchers who studied her. While many of these pioneers were very interested in hypnosis and its relationship to psychic phenomena, they never seemed to realize that hypnosis could be used to train people to tap the sixth sense. Many of the first psychical researchers routinely hypnotized their subjects before testing them, but they never attempted to make any creative use of the state.

This state of affairs was no doubt the result of the way the early parapsychologists viewed psychic ability. They generally believed that ESP was a special talent only possessed by certain very gifted people ... or when someone entered into an extraordinary state of mind such as trance. They did not readily believe that ESP could be linked to our normal waking state. This bias was so strong that when J. B. Rhine instituted his Duke University experiments in the 1930s, he began by routinely hypnotizing his student volunteers before testing them. He only gave up the practice when he discovered that ESP was a widespread ability and that his best subjects could perform well on card-guessing tests no matter what state of mind they were in.

Rhine's discovery that ESP was a normal human potential created a reverse bias among parapsychologists. As interest in testing people for ESP spread, no one bothered to determine if it might be particularly linked to extraordinary states of mind. Hypnosis was not to reemerge as an experimental variable until 1945, and didn't make a formal comeback until the mid-1950s. And it wasn't until the 1960s that the consciousness revolution and the human potentials movement fully alerted parapsychologists to the value of hypnosis and other altered states of consciousness. Yet even before the 1960s, much experimental research had already demonstrated strong links between ESP and the hypnotic state.

One of the most enterprising of these experiments was reported shortly after parapsychology's emergence as an experimental science. John J. Grela was a student at St. Lawrence University in Canton, New York, when he conducted his neat and trim experiment, which is still impressive when evaluated today.

Grela recruited twenty-one subjects for the experiment and began by determining which of them were good hypnotic subjects by how well they performed on a susceptibility test. Eleven individuals were eventually placed in the hypnosis group, while the others were tested with waking suggestions. The experimental procedure was then carried out in four stages. First, the subjects assigned to the hypnosis group were tested individually for ESP by guessing through several runs of ESP cards. These same subjects were later hypnotized and given strong suggestions that they would score well on the same test after being brought out of trance. Then they were retested. In order to judge just how well hypnotic suggestion affects ESP scoring, Grela then hypnotized his experimental participants for a second time. This time they were told that ESP research was a waste of time, though they were requested to cooperate in some further ESP card runs anyway. The last part of the project focused on the ten control subjects, who were tested for ESP after simply receiving strong suggestions to perform well on the upcoming ESP runs.

The overall results of the test showed a great deal of extra-chance scoring. Grela also found that the scores procured from the experimental subjects after they had been given strong positive hypnotic suggestions were higher than their previous control runs. Their scoring after receiving negative suggestions was poor. These results were not earthshaking but they showed an obvious trend indicating how hypnosis could be used to condition experimental subjects into demonstrating ESP.

It seems odd that no one followed up on the Grela work. It used a sleek but effective design, and the results were certainly worth replicating. Nonetheless, it was over ten years before any further research using hypnotic techniques was officially reported, and this work was rather less enterprising.

Jarl Fahler was the next parapsychologist to tackle the tricky subject of hypnosis, and his first report appeared in 1957. Fahler was a Finnish psychologist and worked primarily from his home in Helsingfors. He merely tested several subjects on conventional card-guessing tests both while they were hypnotized and when they were wide awake. His research focused on clairvoyance and precognition, and his subjects tended to score better when under the influence of hypnosis. Once again these results are fairly straightforward, but probably the most notable aspect of Dr. Fahler's work was that none of his subjects were given any sort of hypnotic suggestions to perform well on the tests. They were merely hypnotized and then tested. This would indicate that the subjects performed better because of the state of mind induced by the hypnosis, and not because of any positive expectations that had been instilled in them. Fahler replicated his experiment a year later, but once again made no attempt to actually condition his subjects hypnotically.

The whole issue of using hypnotic suggestion as a conditioning technique wasn't revived until the early 1960s when Dr. Lawrence Casler, then a psychology instructor at Brooklyn College, reported the first of his several hypnotic explorations into the mystery of the sixth sense. Casler worked from the theory that people don't readily display ESP powers either on laboratory tests or in their everyday lives because of their prior social learning. Most of us, Casler argued, have been brainwashed against the possible existence of ESP because of the way we have been taught to view the world by our parents, society, and culture. Casler therefore felt that perhaps hypnotic conditioning might help override this bias. So his research was probably the first to explore a specific theory about how hypnosis can be used as a research tool in parapsychology.

Dr. Casler tested his theory by recruiting forty-eight subjects from among his former students at another New York college. Some of them were placed in the experimental (hypnosis) group, while the others would later be given only waking suggestions. Both groups were tested for clairvoyance and GESP, and each subject was tested individually. After being given instructions to enter the hypnotic state, he or she was given strong suggestions not only that ESP existed, but that they themselves possessed it. The participant was then tested for ESP while remaining under the influence of the hypnosis. A similar set of instructions and suggestions were instilled in the control subjects, who received them while remaining awake. Control runs were also made by the subjects in the hypnosis group while they remained awake for the purpose of comparison.

The results of the project were just as clear-cut as could be. The scores procured from the subjects who had received the waking suggestions were right at chance. So were the scores accumulated from the control runs contributed by the hypnotic subjects. But the scores achieved by the students while they were under the influence of hypnosis were extremely significant.

It is also interesting to note that Casler tried to determine how deeply his subjects were hypnotized by seeing how they responded to hypnotic suggestion. He found no difference between the scoring rates of those who had been lightly hypnotized and those who had been deeply entranced.

Dr. Casler was able to report replications of his seminal work both in 1962 and 1964. It wasn't until 1967, though, that he decided to extend his work by determining whether different types of hypnotic suggestion might variously affect his subjects' ESP scores. He well knew that the hypnotic state is a very personal one, and that hypnotized subjects are very willing and good at offering advice on how they should be treated while entranced. It's not rare, for example, for a hypnotized subject to tell his experimenter the best way to deepen his trance. Keeping this principle in mind, Casler theorized that it might be wise to ask each of his hypnotized subjects just what *kinds* of suggestions for improved ESP scoring they would like administered.

The innovative New York psychologist embarked on this study by enlisting another group of student volunteers. Each was hypnotized and asked to offer suggestions as to what kind of instructions they should be given for better ESP performance. Next they completed four clairvoyance runs with standard ESP cards, after being given suggestions based on their responses. They also completed several runs while awake. The results fully confirmed Casler's earlier results, with the subjects scoring much better in the hypnotic condition than while awake. It is unfortunate, though, that Dr. Casler didn't test to see whether his subjects would also do well on the ESP runs after receiving less personal and more formalized suggestions. These were the very suggestions with which he had so much success a few years earlier. So while provocative, this experiment does not tell us whether personalized suggestions necessarily work any *better* than formal hypnotic conditioning.

Several other attempts to see whether hypnosis was linked to better ESP performance were conducted between 1945–70. The results for many of these tests were positive, and some relationship between ESP and hypnotic conditioning seemed evident. The only problem was that the methodologies employed for these various experiments differed considerably. Some experimental projects were designed to study different parameters of the relationship between hypnosis and ESP. Some studies directly tested whether hypnosis had a direct affect on ESP scoring, while other projects tried to determine whether hypnotic suggestion helped subjects perform *after* they were brought out of trance. Some experiments were meant to determine if hypnotic suggestion affected ESP scoring levels per se, while yet others tested to see if the *state* of hypnosis was conducive to the emergence of ESP. This may seem like a minor point, but please remember that there is a vast chasm between the successful induction of hypnosis and the subject's willingness to actually follow hypnotic suggestion. These two aspects of hypnotic induction are not necessarily linked, since many excellent trance subjects will not follow hypnotic suggestion at all.* It is also important to note that many experimenters tested the same subjects both while hypnotized and while awake. This protocol may have led the participants to expect to perform better on the hypnosis trials. This fact, too, complicates our search to determine the precise relationship between ESP and hypnosis.

In other words, by 1970 there was certainly enough evidence pointing to a link between ESP and hypnosis. But no one really had any idea just what the nature of this link entailed.

The fact that so much confusion exists within the parapsychological community over the relationships between ESP and the hypnotic state shouldn't seem odd. Hypnosis itself constitutes one of conventional psychology's most embarassing enigmas. There is no doubt that it exists, works, and is a powerful therapeutic tool; but psychologists are far from sure how or why. Now this book probably isn't the place to examine the whole controversy surrounding the nature of hypnosis, but you should be aware of the essentials that constitute this debate. There are many schools of thought about the nature of hypnosis, and by understanding these various approaches, some clues about how and why hypnosis seems particularly linked to ESP may become a little clearer to us.

The first thing to keep in mind is that hypnosis is not a discrete state of consciousness. Let me explain this a bit. Both waking and sleeping are discrete states of consciousness since they are accompanied by specific psychophysiological concomitants. When you are awake, for example, your brain produces electrical impulses that can range from 8 to 30 hz per second. These can be recorded by an EEG machine, and any EEG technician looking over your chart will be able to tell that you were awake when the readings were taken. The various stages of sleep are also accompanied by special EEG patterns. When we talk about hypnosis, though, we cannot speak in terms of any single state of consciousness, since hypno-

---

*I can personally testify to this fact. Between 1979 and 1981 I had the chance to hypnotize several UFO "close encounter" witnesses. I found that some of them would readily enter a deep hypnotic state but would be impervious to any attempt to lead them or follow hypnotic suggestion.

sis may range from a very light stage of relaxation to deep somnambulism. The hypnotic state an individual enters after being read an induction procedure may differ greatly from the response of a fellow subject. I have personally had subjects respond to my own induction procedures along a whole gamut of depths. Some have later denied that they were ever really under, while one participant actually lost consciousness altogether. That's quite a range of reactions, yet they were all technically hypnotized. There has recently been some speculation and evidence that the specific depth of the hypnotic state can be monitored by the way the skin alters its capacity to conduct an electrical current, but even this is very tentative and can hardly differentiate formal hypnosis from various levels of simple relaxation. So the only way to truly define hypnosis would be to say that it is "that state in which a person finds himself after being read an hypnotic induction procedure."

This may sound rather facetious, but it is just about the only way to accurately describe hypnosis without someone arguing the point. Even veteran hypnotists often cannot tell the difference between an individual who is genuinely hypnotized and a subject who is simulating the state.

So hypnosis is therefore a very personal state about which we know relatively little. Yet it seems to represent an artifically induced state of altered awareness in which the subject's focus of attention is restricted to his own subjective experiences and to the will of the hypnotist. But just how it differs phenomenologically from other internally focused altered states of consciousness is not very clear.

You may have noted by this time that sometimes I have avoided saying that individuals undergoing hypnosis are in a "trance." The reason is that the word *trance* is rather meaningless. Some psychologists are currently debating whether such a thing as a hypnotic trance even exists. For example, one school of thought believes that the hypnotic condition is actually a state of psychological regression in which the participant voluntarily takes on the needs and fantasies of a child. He relates to the hypnotist as an authority or father figure to whom he subdues his own will. Researchers who promote this line of thinking have little use for a concept as vague as "trance" or an "altered state of consciousness." Not many authorities have followed this line of basically psychoanalytical thinking, however. The most pertinent debate within psychology has long been between those schools of thought promoted by Dr. Ernest Hilgard of Stanford University, who believes in the existence of a discrete hypnotic trance, and the views of T. X. Barber, who believes that hypnosis is merely a behavioral and social response to verbal suggestion which entails no true trance or significant alteration of consciousness. The long debate between these two theories constitutes an enormously important chapter in the history of psychology.

It is Dr. Hilgard's view that hypnosis is a genuine altered state of consciousness which is accompanied by exceptional and discrete subjective phenomenology—including the redistribution of attention, tolerance for reality distortion and role playing, the emergence of fantasy, and the willingness to follow verbal suggestion. He and his followers totally accept the existence of the hypnotic trance. They view it as a natural result of an altered state of consciousness into which the subject descends during the process of induction. To support his view, he points out that hypnotized subjects can readily identify this state as something subjectively different from their normal waking state.

These views and the evidence supporting them have been harshly critized by T. X. Barber, who has reported on several critical experiments he has conducted in Massachusetts. He and his colleagues have shown that most of the classic phenomena of hypnosis, such as arm catalepsy, age regression, the emergence of hallucinations, and imagery, can all be elicited from many people merely by giving them strong verbal suggestions. No hypnosis need be induced. Barber likes to playfully place the word hypnosis in quotation marks to drive home his point that there is nothing truly exceptional about the hypnotic state by which it can be differentiated from waking. It is simply role playing, he argues. He considers hypnosis nothing more than a benign brainwashing procedure in which we make our subjects *think* they are in a trance.

Those psychologists who supported Hilgard's "trance theorist" viewpoint were quick to respond when Barber first started promoting his role-playing model. They argued that Barber and his colleagues may have inadvertently hypnotized their subjects while giving them such strong waking suggestions! Both schools of thought were soon engaged in a mad race to see who could obtain the best evidence for their respective views, but each research report published by one faction was quickly answered by proponents of the other. Neither camp had any problem fitting any new data into their own frameworks. So it can hardly be said that either faction ever won the debate.

The reason for the stalemate is probably because a bit of truth exists in both the "trance theorist" school of thought and the "role playing" concept. I came to this conclusion several years ago while reading all the experimental research that resulted from this great debate. It struck me that both schools of thought were either oversimplifying what we mean in saying that some one is "hypnotized," or were deliberately overstating their cases. Both camps appeared to be using the term as a designation for a particular state of consciousness instead of realizing that hypnosis cannot be phenomenologically defined. In the long view, though, there does appear to be good evidence that *some* people indeed respond to hypnosis so dramatically that they become virtually entranced. (I have personally only seen one subject enter what I could confidently call a genuine trance, but this is beside the point.) A few experimental hypnotists have worked extensively with these subjects and have conducted some highly original research with them. Some of the cleverest of these explorations were the brainchild of the late Milton Erikson, one of the truly great pioneers in the study and application of clinical hypnosis. He found that he could hypnotize some subjects so deeply that they readily responded when he produced total deafness in them through suggestion. He then demonstrated that these deep trance subjects could not be aroused even by attempts to trick them with sudden noises. Another interesting finding is that after being hypnotically regressed, some subjects can recall foreign languages they spoke as very young children; yet they can not recall them when asked to attempt to do so consciously.

That a genuine hypnotic trance probably exists is a logical conclusion to draw from studies such as these. But it is also likely that it is only the most radical stage of what we call hypnosis, and is probably a rare phenomenon. It might also be kept in mind that people vary in their response to hypnotic induction. Entering an hypnotic state may represent a voluntary alteration of attention for some people, while others may voluntarily roleplay in response to the induction procedure. So you might say that altering one's focus of attention and role playing are really merely different *strategies* individuals may use to enter hypnosis. Neither altered awareness nor role playing may actually *define* the hypnotic state.

The role of the subject's own volition is probably the crux of hypnosis, though. Entering the hypnotic state is, according to some experts, really a form of autohypnosis. The role of the therapist or hypnotist is actually to guide you as you draw upon your inner resources while entering an altered state of awareness. You are really doing the work yourself, though there are tricks and maneuvers the hypnotist can use to regulate your adaption to the hypnotic state. This may seem very manipulative, but undergoing hypnosis carries with it the unspoken assumption that you will be actively cooperating with the hypnotist (consciously or unconsciously) as the induction takes place.

With all these issues now clearly in mind, we can return to the subject of ESP and how it is so curiously linked with hypnosis.

No matter to which school of thought you ascribe, it should be clearer now why hypnosis and hypnotic conditioning act as catalysts for the sixth sense. They appear to work because they act on several factors that are known to boost ESP performance. During the course of the last five decades, parapsychologists both in this country and in Europe have uncovered a few rather consistent factors that are directly related to ESP. Included among these are that (a) ESP tends to emerge when attention is focused away from the outside world and redirected internally; (b) that people who believe in ESP perform consistently better on laboratory tests than people who don't; and (c) that people who are strongly convinced that they can do well when tested for ESP outperform people who are hesitant or indifferent. To sum all this up, you might say that a psychic is someone who believes in ESP, has confidence in his or her ability, and knows how to go inward to make contact with the world of subjective experience.

You have probably realized by now how formal hypnosis manipulates all three of these factors. The process of hypnotic induction helps the subject focus away from the distractions of the outside world; there can be little doubt about that. By testing an individual while he or she is hypnotized, we are also subtly manipulating his belief system. Anyone under the influence of deep hypnosis is being implicitly asked to suspend his normal experience of the outside world, and this will include his normal resistance to ESP. This underlying principle probably works in conjunction with our overt suggestions that ESP exists and that he or she will do well when tested. The induction of hypnosis also instills some strong expectancies in our experimental subjects—i.e., that after being subjected to something as weird as hypnosis, they should be able to demonstrate ESP after going through the ritual. So in the long run hypnosis appears to be a multi-faceted procedure in which we subtly reeducate our subjects into being psychic ... at least momentarily.

If the line of reasoning I have just put forth is correct, then it is logical to assume that hypnosis might be a means by which we could actually train people in the use of ESP. This was a potential researchers back in the 1940s and '50s never appreciated. The parapsychological community only began taking this idea seriously in the 1960s when Dr. Milan Ryzl, a biochemist and parapsychologist living in Czechoslovakia, reported that he had successfully trained several gifted subjects through hypnotic conditioning.

Dr. Ryzl, who emigrated to the United States shortly after his work came to international attention, published the fullest description of his method in 1966. There he compartmentalized his training program into five stages. The first stage entails psychologically preparing the subject for the upcoming ESP training program. The participant's motivation is increased during this introductory phase, and emphasis is placed on the seriousness of the project. The nature of hypnosis is also directly discussed with the subject, who is constantly urged to believe that he really can develop ESP powers if he wants to.

The induction of formal hypnosis constitutes the second phase of the training. This is only implemented when the experimenter feels he has broken through any resistances the participant might harbor. Ryzl personally uses an eye fixation technique during which the subject stares at a shiny object while receiving verbal suggestions that he is becoming drowsy. The depth of the hypnosis is of little consequence at this stage of the training. Ryzl himself points out that "it is not necessary to obtain a state of deep hypnosis; on the contrary, the author has found that a state of lighter hypnosis, from which the subject emerges with a memory of what has taken place, is more effective, and that the resulting experience is a favorable basis for further experiments." Ryzl also maintains that by remembering what has happened, the subject appreciates the fact that he has yielded to the influence of the hypnotist. This builds up his confidence in the training program, makes him more comfortable with the hypnotic state, and makes him more willing to follow future suggestions. The only drawback to using such light hypnosis, according to Ryzl, is that some subjects tend to emerge from it spontaneously.

Merely inducing hypnosis is not an end in itself, though. The training also entails teaching the subject to follow verbal suggestions, such as hearing hallucinatory sounds suggested by the experimenter, or experiencing arm catalepsy. The hypnotist becomes very authoritative at this point by constantly pointing out to the subject how subordinated his own will has become to that of the experimenter. These strongly directive suggestions are coupled with promises that the hypnotist's will will grow and grow and will ultimately help the subject acquire ESP abilities.

The most important aspect of this phase of the program is not, however, linked to these directives. The real crux entails training the subject in generating and controlling mental imagery and training his or her powers of visualization. As Ryzl points out,

> Particular attention is paid to the induction of visual hallucinations, which must be as vivid and sharp as if the subject were seeing them with his eyes open. They must be mastered as thoroughly as possible, and the subject must be able to alter them quickly in response to any suggestion, however unexpected. In the example which follows, a hallucination is developed suggestively: the vision of a bouquet of yellow tulips.
>
> The subject chooses a flower. After an appropriate suggestion, it appears to him that the color of the flower is gradually fading and changing to white. He chooses another blossom, whose color gradually changes to orange and finally to red. Another flower will turn to pink. The red blossom may continue to darken, and then turn from crimson to black. We tell the subject to find some lilies-of-the-valley among the tulips; then, by suggestion, we alter the color successively from white to various hues. We allow the subject to smell the flowers. Eventually, he reacts immediately to every wish we express; and the visions will be as constant, as sharp, and as distinct as any normal visual perception...

Only when the subject has perfectly mastered these imagery strategies is he ready to be tested for ESP. The mastery of these imagery skills must also be coupled with a capacity and willingness to follow all of the hypnotist's directions. By this time in the training, Ryzl believes that the subject "has been prepared psychologically to such a degree that in many cases a simple order is sufficient to produce the clairvoyant faculty automatically." Ryzl begins the ESP training with very uncomplicated tasks, such as placing a simple object in front of the participant (whose eyes remain closed through the session) and asking him to describe it.

Ryzl fully appreciated that the subject may succeed ... albeit gropingly or indistinctly at first ... or fail at this point. If the subject fails at his first attempt to use ESP, it is up to the experimenter to explore the reason for the failure and try to help the subject overcome it. Strong verbal suggestions that he or she will eventually develop psychic abilities are coupled with constant encouragement in most cases.

If the subject has demonstrated some beginning ESP ability, though, the training program can go on to the fourth phase, in which the participant is encouraged to develop his psychic talents further. Much time and effort is spent educating the subject about the sources of error that can potentially contaminate the ESP channel. The actual ESP tests are made progressively more difficult, and the subject is taught to focus more consistently on the target, avoid misinterpreting what he "sees," reject random mental imagery arising from his own unconscious, and censor out ESP messages arising from sources other than the target. It is also at this point that the experimenter faces the trickiest aspect of the training. Up until this time the whole strategy behind the training has been to subjugate the will of the participant to that of the hypnotist. This process must now be marginally reversed. If the subject appears to be developing ESP ability, the experimenter must now help him or her take control of the sixth sense. This is done by giving immediate feedback about the accuracy or errors of his psychic perceptions. This feedback allows the subject to learn how to judge when his or her impressions are right or wrong. This not only helps the subject employ ESP efficiency, it also allows him to take responsibility for his or her gifts. Ryzl places strong emphasis on this feedback training.

The fifth stage of the Ryzl method does away with the formal hypnosis completely. The subject is now told that the hypnotic induction is no longer necessary and is encouraged to enter a state of mind conducive to the emergence of ESP voluntarily. The participant is helped to induce a form of autohypnosis and is taught to work in this state without the experimenter's direction.

This entire training program may take up to several months to complete. It takes an extraordinary commitment on the part of both experimenter and participant. It is a rather elaborate system, and only the basics of it have been outlined here.

Apart from the particulars of his system, Dr. Ryzl has also made a series of informal points about the best way to implement it. These are important factors to keep in mind, so they will be summarized in capsule form:

1. Only highly motivated subjects who are good hypnotic subjects should be recruited. Their high level of motivation should not be allowed to wane as the training proceeds.
2. The experiments should not be conducted impersonally or by rote. The special interests of the subject should always be considered. His hobbies, aesthetic likes and dislikes, and so on should help the experimenter choose the nature of the ESP targets and the types of suggestions offered during the training.
3. The subject must absolutely believe that ESP exists. Any vestiges of resistance or doubt will undermine the training.

4. The most crucial part of the training comes when the experimenter advises his subject about the many sources of error that can contaminate ESP vision. The experimenter must work patiently to help his student identify the sources of error he is most likely to encounter as well as help him overcome them.

5. Both the participant and the experimenter must eventually learn when the former has reached a state of consciousness right on the border between waking and sleeping. This is the optimal state of consciousness from which ESP emerges.

Dr. Ryzl has been able to chalk up a number of successes as a result of his program. He issued a report in 1962 on a young Czech named Pavel Stepanek, who claimed that he had never had a psychic experience before entering the program. He apparently worked for several weeks with Dr. Ryzl and developed the impressive ability to determine the color of cards held outside his view. The level of his accuracy was so impressive that researchers from the United States traveled to Prague to study him for themselves. His success on their tests remained so consistently high that he was later brought to this country for further testing at the Institute for Parapsychology in Durham, North Carolina. To date, though, the case of Pavel Stepanek is the only one Dr. Ryzl has brought forward publicly. This has led some researchers to view Ryzl's claims with skepticism.

There have also been several attempts on the part of independent researchers to utilize the Ryzl techniques, but unfortunately, no one has reported very much success with it. Reports were issued from this country, from Cambridge, and from the University of Edinburgh. These failures have led several parapsychologists to dismiss the possible importance of the Ryzl method. It is a debatable point, however, whether any of these investigations really followed the Ryzl method to the point. Some of the researchers only worked with the initial phases of the training and ignored its subtler aspects, while others tested their subjects with conventional card-guessing procedures. Ryzl would have eschewed this approach, since his program is geared toward more free-response imagery. Even experts on the relationship between hypnosis and ESP have not been swayed by these experimental failures. Charles Honorton reexamined the whole issue of ESP and hypnotic conditioning in 1969 and concluded that, "Irrespective of the ultimate verdict on the Ryzl 'training' method, it does not appear that any of the attempts to replicate it have taken *all* of the potentially important aspects of the method into consideration."* Nor have most researchers interested in the Ryzl techniques taken into consideration the very personal manner in which the Czech scientist hypnotized his subjects. From what I have been able to gather from colleagues who have watched him at work, Ryzl uses a very directive and authoritarian approach in which the subject is literally ordered into an altered state of consciousness. This is very different from the approach to clinical hypnosis usually used in this country, whereby the subject is more or less guided and invited into the hypnotic state with soothing suggestions. Ryzl's very directive approach to hypnosis may be a mitigating factor in his success.

The fact that Ryzl's training methods may be a viable approach to psychic development also gains a slender thread of support by the fact that ESP experiments specifically designed to elicit mental imagery from hypnotized subjects have, by and large, fared pretty well. Dr. Stanley Krippner conducted one such experiment at the Maimonides Medical Center's parapsychology lab in which he hypnotized several subjects and then instructed them to take a "nap" right after the session. They were further instructed to dream during this post-hypnotic sleep about a target picture that would be sent to them from another room. The results of the experiment were quite successful. Charles Honorton conducted a similar experiment at the lab a year later. He and a colleague worked with six highly susceptible participants, who were hypnotized and told to "dream" about a picture enclosed in a sealed envelope. The results of the experiment were impressive, but not nearly as significant as the Krippner experiment of 1968.

It should be clear by now that a definite relationship exists between the state of mind or heightened suggestibility induced by hypnosis and ESP. Some subtle interaction between the state of mind induced by the hypnotic induction and how the experimenter's verbal suggestions work on the subject's belief system and expectancy is the likely root of this relationship. So despite the complexities of the hypnotic state, formal hypnosis is probably one method for helping people make contact with their psychic potentials that has had the widest and most consistent success.

It therefore seems odd that very little research has explored the possible links between ESP and self-hypnosis. Such a relationship would seem fairly obvious. Ryzl's method culminates when the participant learns how to enter a deep hypnagogic state of altered consciousness

---

*Only one further attempt to replicate the Ryzl work has been reported since 1969. It, too, failed.

without the use of formal hypnotic induction. This is essentially a form of self-hypnosis. But no experimental projects have ever been conducted in which subjects proficient in the art of self-hypnosis were specifically tested for ESP.* Why this oversight has gone on for so long is a mystery, since this is a potentially significant area of research. There is considerable evidence that self-hypnotized subjects can act upon any suggestions they may care to give themselves, so ESP might well be elicited from this state as well.

LEARNING SELF-HYPNOSIS

Whole books have been written on inducing and using self-hypnosis. There are innumerable techniques, some designed for immediate self-induction and some systems that can only be mastered after two or three days of work. If you decide to learn self-hypnosis, which method will work best for you will depend on you yourself, since people differ in their susceptibility to autohypnosis just as they do to formal hypnosis. Most systems for self-inducing a hypnotic state are fairly consistent, however. They usually address themselves to four stages of conditioning including (1) relaxation, (2) trance induction, (3) strategies for deepening the state, and (4) strategies for self-suggestion. The latter procedures are usually geared toward dealing with such common problems as smoking, lack of self-confidence, anxiety over work or school, poor study habits, and similar nettling but not overly serious everyday situations. Even many clinical hypnotherapists end their program of treatment by teaching their clients how to hypnotize themselves. This way the patient can reinforce the conditioning he or she has received at periodic intervals.

Systems for inducing self-hypnosis can be broken down into three major approaches. These consist of tape-recorded instruction methods, quick application techniques, and prolonged formal systems. The latter differs from the former by making use of more extensive training programs in self-suggestion. They also spend more time teaching strategies for greater trance depth and skills. You should try experimenting with all of

*The only exception is an experiment reported by two researchers at Washington and Jefferson College (Washington, Pa.) who tested a single subject. Michael V. Novinski and Joseph A. Wineman reported to the 1978 Southeast Regional Parapsychological Association that a selected subject proficient in self-hypnosis had guessed the suits on playing cards to an extraordinary degree after inducing deep relaxation.

these methods before deciding which works best for you. After you have successfully learned hypnotic self-induction, though, you might find that you can freely interchange these various approaches. Learning self-hypnosis is like learning any other skill. It becomes easier and easier the more time you spend with it.

If you are a little wary of trying to learn self-hypnosis, tape-recorded induction techniques are obviously the easiest to implement, and work well for people who have a difficult time voluntarily abandoning themselves to internally focused states of awareness. People who like to follow rather than lead do well with this approach to self-hypnosis. Many metaphysical bookstores and self-help organizations sell self-hypnosis tapes geared toward home use and for developing skills that can be applied toward more autonomous autohypnosis. A variety of tape programs are marketed by the Sutphen Corporation (Box 38, Malibu, California 90265) on the west coast. Many of their tapes are specifically designed for people who take a metaphysical view of life. You can couple any of these tapes with self-suggestions for better ESP performance. You can then test yourself with any of the types of ESP tests outlined earlier in this book.

If you really want to learn autohypnosis, though, you should learn to induce the state by relying solely on your own inner resources. So many systems have been worked out to self-induce the hypnotic trance it would be too unwieldy to outline them all. What follows is actually a rather eclectic approach which I have drawn from several different texts and systems, and which can be especially geared toward quick induction. There really is nothing novel about the following procedures since they are based on commonly employed strategies taught by most authorities on the subject.

Self-inducing a hypnotic state is not really that difficult. It basically entails quieting the mind through various mental and physical exercises:

1. Find a quiet place where you won't be disturbed. This is absolutely essential for inducing self-hypnosis, even more so than it was for engaging in relaxation exercises and the like.
2. Dim the lights in the room and then sit in a comfortable chair or lie down.
3. Put yourself through an entire program of systematic progressive muscular relaxation. This will prepare both the mind and the body for the eventual induction of hypnosis.
4. Fix your eyes on a single point in the room. This should be right at your line of vision or a little above it so that you will have to squint a bit (but not strain) upwards. You can also focus on a bright object of some sort, such as a candle flame. Try not to move your eyes from the spot as you proceed.

5. Give yourself a series of mental suggestions that your eyes are becoming heavier and heavier with each breath you take. You can improvise freely at this point. You can suggest that you are getting sleepy, that your eyelids are like weights, or anything else you find effective. The basic strategy is to repeat these instructions until you really can't keep your eyes open any longer, but do not doze off when you close them. Remind yourself constantly that once your eyes close, you will be hypnotized.

If you find your eyes closing at this point, you will have successfully entered a light hypnotic state. You shouldn't go any further than this during your first or second session. Just get used to feeling the sensations of entering into an internally focused state of consciousness. Rousing yourself should present no problem. Merely tell yourself that you are going to count backwards from ten to one, and that you will gradually awake as you reach the end of the countdown. Constantly reinforce this suggestion as you count, interrupting the recitation in order to remind yourself that you will be invariably emerging from your hypnotic state as you count.

Hypnosis and self-hypnosis are slow processes to master, so don't try to do too much each session. Begin by learning only to induce a self-hypnotic state. Learning to *use* the hypnotic state will come later.

You might find that this eye-fixation system doesn't work too well for you, especially at first. If you are having problems with it, you might use an alternate strategy. One of my own favorites is the metronome technique. Set a metronome clicking at a slow and steady rate. Begin the induction process by following the initial steps outlined above, but instead of fixing your eyes on a point in space or on a bright object, just stare up at the ceiling. Give yourself repeated suggestions that your eyes are getting heavier and heavier as each click of the metronome recurs and that you will enter trance when they close. Repeat the suggestions to yourself until you find your eyes beginning to close. This technique is very effective since any monotonous stimulus hitting the brain for any prolonged period of time quiets it and causes a sleep response. Just ask anyone who has listened to some one practicing piano scales over and over! You won't fall asleep, though, because you will be actively giving yourself the alternate suggestion to enter a hypnotic condition.

The metronome technique can also be used in conjuction with eye-fixation procedures. You can use the metronome's incessant clicking to underlie the suggestion that your eyes are becoming heavier and heavier. You can use this instead of relying on your breath to set up this reinforcement schedule.

It can't be stressed enough that the most important part of any induction procedure is repetition. The brain and mind simply cannot resist repeated suggestions for very long. The suggestions eventually register deep within the subconscious. This is, in fact, the whole basis for the phenomenon of hypnotic suggestion. It is important to remember not to try too hard when you begin, though. Learning to hypnotize yourself is a skill that you must gradually develop. Work steadily and slowly until you find yourself easily following your own suggestions.

Another problem with which the beginning student is often concerned is how to recognize when he or she is actually hypnotized. This is a tricky area since, as I explained earlier, everyone's experience of hypnosis is bound to be slightly different. Since hypnosis can be defined roughly as a heightened state of suggestibility, the fact that your eyes have closed as a result of your self-instructions is a prima facie indication that you are hypnotized. If you prefer to demonstrate or prove to yourself that you are actually hypnotized, you might test yourself by the use of some self-hypnotic suggestions. See how well you follow them. This actually entails placing yourself in a deeper trance than you have implemented as a result of your initial induction. So this phase of your self-training should not be undertaken without first having total mastery of the initial induction phase. Then you can really get down to work.

The first way to determine to your own statisfaction that you have indeed taught yourself to enter a hypnotized state is to deepen the state voluntarily. This not only places you in a state of mind where you will probably have easier access to your ESP potentials (at least according to the Ryzl method), but you will also be able to mentally "feel" yourself descending deeper and deeper into mental passivity. This is a very effective way of demonstrating that you are no longer truly awake.

Deepening the hypnotic state is very simple once you have initially entered trance. There are a number of techniques you can use and you should experiment with several of them in order to find the one that works best for you. The most elementary one is the "count down" procedure, in which you give yourself suggestions for deeper trance over and over again as you count from one to ten. Simply count progressively, interrupting your counting often in order to reinforce the association between trance depth and the numbers. For example, the following is the type of self-suggestions you might use at this point in your training:

I am going to count from one to ten. As I count, I shall go deeper and deeper into my hypnotic trance. I can't help becoming more and more relaxed as I count. Each number draws me further down into the hypnotic state ... progressively and consistently. One ... Two ... already I feel myself falling deeper and deeper asleep. Three ... yes, I'm feeling much more relaxed and will continue to do so as I count. Four ... Five ... I'm now so deeply entranced that I can hardly rouse myself. My only thought is how to go even deeper. Six ... I'm even deeper now. It feels so good to be so relaxed. Seven ... Eight ... I'm almost to my ultimate point of total relaxation. It is so easy to become so relaxed. Nine ... Ten ... I am now so totally relaxed and entranced that I will unfailingly follow any further suggestions I give myself.

Another common technique for deepening the hypnotic state is to envision yourself walking down a flight of stairs or a spiral staircase. Picture this vividly in your mind. Constantly tell yourself that you will become more and more entranced as you descend the stairs. Speed up the repetition of these suggestions as you picture yourself reaching the bottom.

By this time you should be able to subjectively determine at what level of hypnosis you are functioning. Subjectively identifying when you are hypnotized and are functioning at either a light or deep stage is a totally valid way of determining your state of mind. If you are a naturally born skeptic, however, you still want objective proof that you have really entered an extraordinary state of consciousness. There is no better way than by experimenting with self-suggestion. If you have successfully entered a deep hypnotic state, you should be able to follow your own suggestions. Here are a few tasks you can try:

1. Give yourself the command that your eyes are glued shut and that you can't open them no matter how hard you try. Repeat this suggestion over and over. Then actively attempt to open them. If you are able to open them this only means that you will have to practice some more to accomplish the proper depth of hypnosis.

   I personally don't recommend this task at first, since it is a little discouraging if you fail. It can also potentially disrupt the hypnotic state. Remaining hypnotized yet functioning with your eyes open is possible, but can only be accomplished by a skilled practitioner. It isn't too advisable to attempt this during the early stages of training. Opening your eyes during the state of self-hypnosis can also bring you back to full awareness spontaneously, which should of course be avoided.

2. A better task is to repeat over and over that your arm is getting lighter and lighter and that you simply cannot keep it from floating up and away from your body. This is called the "arm levitation" technique and is a very common way of convincing people that they are really hypnotized. You might have to repeat the suggestion for several minutes, but if the hypnotic state is deep enough, you will invariably be successful.

3. An alternate technique is to suggest to yourself that your arm is getting heavier and heavier and you cannot raise it no matter how hard you try.

Once you have found that you can respond to these types of hypnotic suggestion, you are now ready to direct your newfound talent toward the possibility of learning better psychic functioning. Before proceeding, though, *always be sure to remove each and every suggestion you have given yourself so that it will not carry over into the waking state after you have roused yourself.*

To program yourself for tapping into your psychic potentials, you should initiate a three-stage series of conditioning suggestions:

1. Begin by telling yourself that ESP exists. Give yourself a little talk on how you know that ESP is a reality and how ridiculous it is to deny or reject this simple fact. Also tell yourself that you have no resistance, either psychologically or emotionally, against the idea that psychic capacities are real. Especially instruct your unconscious mind that it will release you from any ingrained beliefs that might inhibit you from accepting the reality of telepathy, clairvoyance, precognition, and mind over matter.

2. Don't go on to this stage until your next conditioning session, since you want to give your mind a little time to assimilate the suggestions you have just given yourself. Now you can proceed by telling yourself that you, too, have ESP powers just like everyone else does. Tell yourself that you can use your psychic potentials at will, and that by entering hypnosis, you can voluntarily tap into your psychic capabilities. Suggest that your mind is free from all restrictions of time and space, and that your unconscious mind will obey you when you instruct it to latch onto any piece of psychic information you wish to receive.

3. You can now actually test yourself for ESP. Choose a specific psychic task, such as calling through a deck of ESP cards or clairvoyantly peering into a sealed envelope where a pictorial target has been placed. Remind yourself how easy it is to succeed at this task, and that no obstacles can keep you from tapping directly into the information you need. Order your unconscious mind to bring forth the proper images on the cards or those that reflect the picture.

It might be helpful to prepare tapes making these various suggestions. You can then play the tapes at the appropriate time after you have induced a deep state of hypnosis. Most authorities on autohypnosis encourage the use of prepared tapes so that you can hear any important suggestions you wish to act upon as though they are coming from an outside source. This works very effectively since you are in a highly suggestion-prone state.

Hypnosis and self-hypnosis can be applied to any of the types of ESP self-testing programs and experiments that were outlined in the previous chapters. You can test yourself with ESP cards, pictorial free-response material, or devise your own tests. Another approach you can use is one drawn from the Ryzl system. Ask a friend to place five small but very distinct objects in a series of small boxes. Keep these next to you when you hypnotize yourself, and then try to determine what object is in each box. Don't necessarily try to specifically name the object. That task is too analytical to attempt while you are in an altered state of consciousness. Try to focus in on the object's form, texture, color, and so on. You might tape-record your impressions for each target and then see if your friend can determine which description matches which object. Or you can have your friend remove the objects from the boxes and then you can try to make the matchups yourself.

Self-hypnosis can be used not only to enter an ESP-conducive state of mind, but also to reeducate yourself about the reality of ESP and your ability to make use of this mysterious capability. Therefore you should not remove any of your suggestions about the existence of ESP or your capacity to use it at the conclusion of each of your sessions. To the contrary, you should end each session with specific post-hypnotic suggestions that you are becoming more and more psychic the longer you practice, and that every time you hypnotize yourself, you will be that much more psychically gifted.

Learning to induce and use autohypnosis is, however, probably the most complicated strategy for potentially developing ESP ability. The few suggestions that have been offered here hardly do justice to this fascinating area of psychology. If you choose to use self-hypnosis as your individual strategy, you should read and study several manuals on its proper use, and experiment with many different techniques for deepening the state, for giving yourself suggestions, and for implementing post-hypnotic suggestions. The advantages of learning self-hypnosis go beyond just trying to learn psychic functioning, however, since there are many uses to which the skill can be put to use. So you won't be wasting your time learning the art, even if you eventually find another ESP strategy that works better for you.

Be aware, though, that more nonsense has been written on self-hypnosis than on practically any other self-improvement skill. Be careful just what manuals you use as your guide. The late Leslie LeCron wrote several books on hypnosis and self-hypnosis that are fairly reliable. Ronald Shone's recent book *Autosuggestion—a step-by-step guide to self-*

hypnosis offers excellent practical advise on trance induction. He tends to offer some very naive views on how self-hypnosis is related to brain hemispheric lateralization, but these editorial remarks do not detract from the value of the exercises he suggests. A more elaborate and time-consuming program for learning self-hypnosis is given by Dr. Freda Morris in her *Self-Hypnosis in Two Days.* Both of these books are cited in the references.

References

Casler, Lawrence. The improvement of clairvoyance scores by means of hypnotic suggestion. *Journal of Parapsychology,* 1962, *26,* 77–87.

Casler, Lawrence. The affects of hypnosis on GESP. *Journal of Parapsychology,* 1964, *28,* 126–34.

Casler, Lawrence. Self-generated hypnotic suggestions and clairvoyance. *International Journal of Parapsychology,* 1967, *9,* 125–8.

Fahler, Jarl. ESP card tests with and without hypnosis. *Journal of Parapsychology,* 1957, *21,* 179–85.

Grela, John J. Effects of ESP scoring on hypnotically induced attitudes. *Journal of Parapsychology,* 1945, *9,* 194–202.

Honorton, Charles and Krippner, Stanley. Hypnosis and ESP: a review of the experimental literature. *Journal* of the American Society for Psychical Research, 1969, *63,* 175–84.

Honorton, Charles and Stump, John. A preliminary study of hypnotically-induced clairvoyant dreams. *Journal* of the American Society for Psychical Research, 1969, *63,* 175–84.

Inglis, Brian. *Natural and Supernatural.* London: Hodder & Stoughton, 1977.

Krippner, Stanley. Experimentally-induced telepathic effects in hypnosis and non-hypnosis groups. *Journal* of the American Society for Psychical Research, 1968, *62,* 387–98.

Morris, Freda. *Self-hypnosis in Two Days.* New York: Dutton, 1974.

Myers, F. W. H. On telepathic hypnotism and its relation to other forms of hypnotic suggestion. *Proceedings* of the Society for Psychical Research, 1886, *4,* 129–37.

Novinski, Michael V. and Wineman, Joseph A. Relaxation through hypnosis and ESP scoring. *Journal of Parapsychology,* 1978, *42,* 60–61.

Parker, Adrian. *States of Mind.* New York: Taplinger, 1975.

Pratt, J. G. A decade of research with a selected ESP subject: an overview and reappraisal of the work with Pavel Stepanek. *Proceedings* of the American Society for Psychical Research, 1973, *30*, 1–78.

Rogo, D. Scott. Research on psi-conducive states: some complicating factors. *Journal of Parapsychology*, 1976, *40*, 34–45.

Ryzl, Milan. A method of training in ESP. *International Journal of Parapsychology*, 1966, *8*, 501–32.

Sargent, Carl. Hypnosis as a psi-conducive state: a controlled replication study. *Journal of Parapsychology*, 1978, *42*, 257–75.

Shone, Ronald. *Autosuggestion—a step-by-step guide to self-hypnosis.* Wellingborough, Northamptonshire: Thorsons, 1982.

5

the role
of feedback

All through this book, the word "learning" has been used. Can one *learn* to control psychic ability? Can one *learn* to develop psychic talents? Can one *learn* to recognize paranormal impressions when they enter the mind? These are some of the many questions we've been considering during the course of these pages. But never once has the word *learning* been formally defined. Psychologists define learning as "a relatively permanent change in behavior that occurs as the result of practice." Notice that the key word here is *practice.* Most popular books on psychic development, as well as commercially available courses which claim to help the reader or client "learn" psychic abilities, do not stress practice. They tend to merely set forth a series of techniques which are supposed to lead to the automatic development of psychic powers when followed like acookbook recipe. And this is where these books and courses probably go astray, since there can be no true learning without practice. This simple fact has led a few parapsychologists to experiment with the idea that one might be able to develop ESP if this talent were nurtured similarly to the way one learns any skill—i.e., through practice, trial, and error. The results of this research have been promising. Exciting experiments have recently been conducted at two top parapsychology laboratories, and they seem to point the way to a method of making ESP at least more consistent. This in itself is no mean feat!

For years parapsychologists have faced the apparent fact that ESP isn't very reliable. Not only are psychic impressions usually fleeting, fragmented, and distorted by the time they enter the conscious mind, but even gifted psychics often cannot tell when their "impressions" are right or wrong. ESP is a hopelessly unreliable information channel, which is the reason few scientists—even those who readily admit its reality—have bothered to study it. It is also disconcerting to know that most really talented ESP subjects usually *lose* their abilities the more often they are tested in the laboratory. This finding was first made back in the 1930s by J. B. Rhine during his Duke University experiments. It wasn't long before he noted that his subjects tended to do better at the beginning of an experiment than toward the end. But what really disheartened him was how even his best subjects gradually lost *all* their abilities after weeks and months of continual testing.

The so-called "decline effect" has been one of parapsychology's most consistent and embarassing findings. It also indicates that ESP is not a skill that is learned or enhanced merely through repetition. But now—for the first time in the short history of the field—a few parapsychologists are uncovering techniques that may not only prevent subjects from losing their ESP powers, but may actually help them to enhance them. The strategy seems to be a ridiculously obvious and simple one. The key seems to be *feedback*, a basic element of any learning procedure, but one rarely used in parapsychology.

The first indications that people can be trained to score well on ESP tests through the application of learning theory was the result of some research by Russell Targ, until recently a physicist at the Stanford Research Institute in Menlo Park, California, and his colleague David Hurt, a senior applications engineer with Fairchild Microwave and Opto Electronics. Targ and Hart built what they called an "ESP Teaching Machine" in the early 1970s and they presented the results of their first experiments at the Institute of Electrical and Electronic Engineers' (IEEE) International Symposium on Information Theory in 1972. They claimed that, by allowing subjects to test themselves with the machine, they had actually induced ESP learning.

At first glance the machine does not appear to be very complicated. It is merely a box with four buttons on its front panel. Each button is connected to a light and the machine randomly chooses which of the four lights will be the target for each trial. If the subject pushes the correct button, the light will illuminate. So, of course, the subject has a twenty-five percent likelihood of getting a "hit" on each guess he makes. Also included is a pass button. If the subject does not feel that he is getting valid "psychic impressions" for a given trial, he can bypass it and wait for the machine to choose another one. That way the subject is never *forced* to make a decision. All the scores are automatically recorded, and a permanent record of the experiment is punched out within the machine.

The other novel feature of the device is what one could call "ego-boosting" lights. If the subject begins to guess above chance, lights begin to flash noting either "ESP Ability Present" or "Useful at Las Vegas."

What do Targ and Hurt hope to achieve with this machine? "... Our hypothesis," they stated at the IEEE Symposium, "is that enhancement can be accomplished by allowing the user of the machine to become consciously aware of his own mental state at those times when he is most successfully employing his extra-sensory faculties. With increased conscious awareness of his mental state, we believe that he is then able to bring his otherwise intermittent faculties under his volitional control."

Later in the presentation the authors added:

> Because the user obtains immediate information feedback as to the correct answer, he is able to recognize his mental state at those times when he has made a correct response. If the information feedback to the user were not immediate, we believe no mind learning would take place and less or no enhancement would be achieved.

Targ and Hurt's theory did have some confirmation. Although many of their subjects did not increase their ESP performances after training with the machine, a few dramatically improved. One subject steadily increased his ESP scoring over 1600 trials with the machine, while another subject scored 40 correct hits out of 96 trials on three occasions. This is about twice above chance expectation.

The Targ-Hurt ESP trainer can also be manipulated to test subjects for more than just clairvoyance. By making a subtle mechanical change within the circuitry of the device, the apparatus can be altered so that the targets are selected *after* the subject makes his guesses. By working with this revision, subjects undergoing ESP training can be taught to hone their precognitive skills. Targ and Hurt reported to the IEEE that one of their subjects seemed particularly adept at this precognitive task. Not only did she score better and better the more she used the machine, but she was eventually able to identify when she was merely guessing and when she was really using her ESP. This all represents a dramatic change from the typical scoring decline most subjects show after they have been continually tested, and which most parapsychologists have confronted as the dolorous outcome of their experiments.

Nonetheless, the Targ-Hurt work does leave one important question unanswered. Why did only selected subjects successfully learn to use ESP? Why didn't everyone improve after training on the machine?

The answer to this question may be forthcoming from another California-based laboratory. The work of Dr. Charles T. Tart at the University of California at Davis followed closely on the heels of the Targ-Hurt work and ended up exploring the whole issue of ESP learning in greater and more sophisticated detail.

Dr. Tart is probaly one of the most original and versitile psychologists in the United States. He is a pioneer in the clinical study of hypnosis, a leading authority on psychedelic drugs, the first parapsychologist in modern times to study the out-of-body experience in the laboratory, and recently completed a major study on ESP learning. This project has shed valuable light on how learning theory can make a useful contribution to parapsychology. His results also hold out the promise that ESP can be taught and learned just like any other skill.

Dr. Tart's theory that you can teach at least some people to be psychic goes back to 1966 when he published a paper in the *Journal* of the American Society for Psychical Research in which he severely questioned the whole way ESP testing is normally conducted. This was during the heyday of the ESP card-guessing craze. Subjects were routinely asked to guess through a pack of ESP cards and were never told how well they had done until they were finished. As a psychologist familiar with learning theory, Tart argued that such a procedure was bound to prevent even gifted subjects from getting insight into the nature of their abilities ... insights which could help them to improve those abilities. His basic premise was that such protocol did nothing to help subjects *learn* by their successes and their mistakes.

As I mentioned earlier, learning is defined in psychology as "a relatively permanent change in behavior that occurs as the result of practice." In other words, learning takes place when you try something, succeed or fail at it, and then try it over and over again until you succeed regularly. The key to learning is feedback. You must be told or realize *immediately* whether you have succeeded or failed at the task you are attempting to master so that you can try to do better the next time.

Note that this is exactly what conventional ESP testing *doesn't* do. A typical person taking an ESP test is forced to guess blindly over and over again. He or she is never given a chance to know when he is right or just "guessing" at the targets until some later time. As Tart pointed out in 1966, such a process normally leads to the opposite of learning, i.e., extinction. This, he believed, may be the reason for the infamous "decline effect" found by so many researchers. It is Tart's theory that this unfortunate state of affairs resulted because the tests at which the subjects were asked to succeed actually sabotaged their abilities. They should have been told whether they were right or wrong after each and every trial. Such a procedure may have helped them identify any intuitive feelings or other subtle mental manifestations that could have conceivably cued them as to when they were hitting right on target. This is all pretty much identical to what Targ and Hurt were saying, although Tart placed the principle squarely within the paradigm of formal learning theory.

"When you ask somebody to use ESP," Tart explains, "I think an intelligent reaction would be something like, 'Huh? What do you mean you want me to use ESP?' It's not like asking somebody to lift their hand or to say a word. It's not like some task that's been well practiced when they've been trained in a feedback way so they get mighty accurate on it. We forget that we had to learn to use our bodies when we were infants. We had to learn coordination. We learned in the feedback situation that if we reached for something we either got it or we didn't. When we test somebody for using ESP, by and large, the subject hasn't the slightest idea what to do. Should I wrinkle my brow? Should I think of the clear white light hovering two inches to the left of my ear? Should I concentrate on my Chakras? What in the world *do* you do to make ESP work: Well, you don't *know* what to do. You may know what other people say you *ought* to do, but you don't know whether that's accurate. Or some procedures might work for them but not for you."

It is here that the all-important role of feedback comes into play. As Tart also explains:

> If you get feedback information you can try different things and find out what works for you. Maybe picturing the clear white light is a way that would make your ESP wrong, inevitably. You may find you are 100% wrong when you do that, whereas maybe if you wiggle your toes while you're trying to get an ESP impression, that may seem to work a lot of times. That doesn't sound very spiritual, but if that's what works for you, that's what you're going to find through feedback, and you should go with it.

Being an experimentalist by training, Tart is more interested in research than theoretical discussion. So in the early 1970s he initiated a systematic project to see if he could train people to enhance their ESP through the application of simple learning theory.

The psychologist implemented his research with the aid of two machines. The first was the commercially available Aquarius Model 100 ESP Trainer, which was slightly modified for the tests and which is almost identical to the Targ-Hurt trainer. The machine consists of a box on which four geometrical targets are displayed. Each has a button near it. When the machine is activated, it randomly selects one of the shapes and this information is stored within its circuitry. The subject guesses at the target by pushing the button next to the target he feels has been chosen. He may also pass on the trial if he doesn't feel sure of himself. If he guesses correctly, the target panel will light up and a chime will ring. The machine also keeps track of the subject's overall score as he guesses trial after trial, and this is indicated on a separate illuminated read-out display. If the subject does well, special panels at the top of the console will light up, flashing on encouraging statements from "Good beginning" to "outstanding ESP ability." Tart's other machine was his own 10-Choice Trainer Machine which he especially constructed for these studies. The main console consists of a circular display of ten pilot lights next to ten different playing card faces. When activated, the subject merely has to press a button next to the card he thinks has been chosen as the target. The appropriate light will illuminate and a chime will go off if his guess is correct. The 10-Choice Trainer was also especially built, unlike the Aquarius, for telepathy experiments. A duplicate console can be placed in another room and electrically connected to the subject's board. An agent or experimenter at the distant location can not only choose the targets, but can also watch his subject's responses over a TV monitor and help guide him to the correct target psychically.

In order to find potential subjects for his project, Tart sent his assistants out among the student population of the University of California at Davis. They were instructed to test anyone who might wish to try their luck with the machines. Those subjects who scored well on the screening project were then invited to undergo more formal training and testing, since it was Tart's belief that the ability to learn ESP may be easier for people who already possess at least some talent.

It is important to remember that Tart did not theorize that just anyone could learn ESP. He has long believed that a subject can only learn to improve his psychic potentials if he or she already has some trace of ability to begin with. In this respect, he feels that ESP is a talent somewhat like singing or some related musical ability. All of us can carry a tune or croak out a song, he explains, but only a few of us have enough base talent or ability capable of being honed into a fine art. These were the people the California psychologist was interested in discovering and working with in his laboratory.

He eventually found twenty-five potentially gifted subjects who completed a lengthy series of tests on the learning machines. What he discovered was interesting, to say the least. Some of the students did, in fact, improve rather steadily during the course of the testing. So in this respect these lucky students *learned* to do better. Some of them did so well that their ESP scores represent some of the highest reported in parapsychology to date! But what really impressed Dr. Tart was that most of the subjects, while not actually improving, didn't get any worse. They seemed to use the training procedure to stabilize their abilities. This was in striking contrast to the findings of most other researchers who usually found even their best subjects gradually doing worse and worse as time and testing went on. Tart believes that this stabilizing effect is an important breakthrough.

Even so, he is cautious about any conclusions that might be drawn on the basis of his research so far. When I personally asked him in 1981 whether he felt that his research demonstrated a learning effect, he was quite reticent.

"I wish I could say it has, but it's not conclusive as yet," he said. "I have some hints that some people can learn, but I don't have enough of that to give or make a strong scientific statement yet that people can learn ESP."

Nontheless, Tart does believe that the feedback helped his subjects succeed at the tests by helping them learn to identify internal cues which signified when they were using ESP or just guessing.

"Some of my people seemed to get cues that worked at least some of the time," he told me during our conversation. "One woman, for instance, would look for faint patterns of light around the board pointing toward the correct target. Now there weren't any patterns of light there, so this was her own internal process, but for her that was a useful indication. Somebody else would run her hand around the possible targets and she would say it would either feel like fire or like ice. It would feel like *fire* when she was over the correct target, but when she was ready to push a button that was wrong, it felt icy. That would *tell* her it was wrong. Feeling of heat for her was a cue that was helpful."

These early experiments were written up by Dr. Tart in a monograph, *The Application of Learning Theory to Extrasensory Perception*, published in 1975 by the Parapsychology Foundation in New York. Later he expanded his reports and ideas in his controversial book *Learning to Use Extrasensory Perception*. Since that time, Tart has been able to replicate his entire project, once again using university students as his subjects.

These results, which were published in 1979 in the *Journal* of the American Society for Psychical Research, once again showed hints and suggestions that feedback helps people gain some control over their ESP capabilities. But definite proof of a learning effect remained annoyingly elusive. One of the problems with this major follow-up study was that Tart and his colleagues had a difficult time finding subjects who could pass the screening procedures by scoring well with the teaching machines. Only seven students were selected and formally trained and tested with the 10-Choice Trainer, while three were tested with the Aquarius. Those subjects who worked with the 10-Choice Trainer failed to do very well on the subsequent testing, but all three of the subjects working with the Aquarius showed stabilized ESP performance during the rest of the project. It is Tart's personal feeling that both his research team and his subjects were less enthusiastic about this phase of the research, which may have led to the poorer showing. He had to dolorously admit at the conclusion of his report that, "the results of this experiment neither add nor detract from the status of the learning theory" and still points to the outcome of his first study as support for his theory that ESP may be a learned skill.

Important though lab work may be, the results of Dr. Tart's work, no matter how ambiguous his overall findings may seem, do suggest that there are ways that just about anyone could enhance ESP skills and use them in *daily life* as well.

Tart believes that learning some sort of control over the elusive sixth sense is one of parapsychology's most important goals. Our understanding of ESP, he points out, is basically the same as the understanding science had of electricity years ago. The scientists of yesteryear had little understanding of a force that could only manifest itself as wild, strong effects—such as lightning—or small effects seen through static charges. Then someone invented the battery and electricity was harnessed. Parapsychologists face the same dilemma. All the researcher has to work with are uncontrolled displays of powerful ESP—such as occur in daily life or that are produced by great psychics—or the rather weak statistical effects found during laboratory testing. It is Tart's hope that learning procedures might lead to the discovery of a controllable ability. Parapsychologists would then have their psychic "battery."

Today, only a couple of years after the completion of his ESP learning project, Tart has gone on to new interests and projects. He is interested in exploring precognition and would like to conduct more experimental research on the out-of-body experience, which he pioneered back in the 1960s. But he eventually hopes to follow up on his learning work and discover better ways of helping people to use this capricious ability.

"I would like to be able to find some people with moderate talent," he explains, "and then try a lot of variations on this basic learning procedure. For instance, how many target choices should you have? Should you be relaxed? Should you be excited? What kind of personality would be best? Should you have introspective people? Should you have outgoing people? What kind of reward system is best? Is the task its own reward? Should you get money, special praise, or encouragement for doing exceptionally well? There are a lot of practical dimensions like this to solve. How do you put this learning procedure in the best psychological framework? There's lots and lots to do. Basically, I want to find out if I can take people and with this feedback train them to be able to demonstrate strong ESP day in and day out. If I can train people to do that, a total revolution is possible."

It is rather unfortunate that the parapsychological community has, in general, been rather slow to follow up on the leads outlined by Dr. Tart's work. Despite the fact that many researchers, especially those engaged in ganzfeld and other sorts of "free response" testing, are interested in making ESP more consistent and reliable, there have been no formal replications of the Tart work. Other researchers have been openly critical of Dr. Tart's conclusions. He has been criticized for not explaining just what "talent threshhold" a subject must possess before being gifted enough to learn better control of his or her ESP. He has also been lambasted for claiming that he has uncovered evidence for ESP learning when his results do not show the typical types of learning curves psychologists normally see when training their subjects in more conventional skills.

Nonetheless, there remains some tentative evidence that feedback, even if we divorce it from conventional learning theory, may be a legitimate strategy for ESP learning. Some recent work by William Braud carried out at the Mind Science Foundation certainly points in this direction, since he is one of the few researchers who have applied feedback training within the context of free-response experimentation.

Dr. Braud and his assistant, Robert Wood, decided to study whether feedback might help their subjects score better during ganzfeld ESP testing. They utilized the services of 30 volunteers. Each of the subjects was individually escorted to a special test room where they were allowed to lie down on a waterbed where a ganzfeld setting, complete with earphones and ping-pong ball goggles, was prepared for them. Each was tested for ESP during a five-minute sending period during which an agent in another room at the Foundation focused on and tried to send a target picture. The subject was then shown the target picture along with three random ones and tried to identify which of them had been sent during the test.

The catch to this series of tests was that some of the subjects were only tested twice in the ganzfeld. They were tested once to introduce them to the procedure and then completed a follow-up session conducted under the same conditions as the first one. But several of the subjects were allowed to participate in four "practice" sessions in between the two formal sessions, and these were specially designed to help them "learn" to perform better while in the ganzfeld. These practice trials were run along the same lines as the other ones, though for these experiments two target pictures were sent at different times during the session. A bell tone signaled over the headphones alerted the subject when each target was being actively sent. Of course, the experimenter in charge kept a record of the subject's mentation during the test. The agent who was trying to send the target theme was *also* able to hear the subject's report over an intercom hooked to his station. If the subject seemed to be describing something represented on the target picture, the agent could signal him by sending a special tone over the headset. In this way, the subjects received instant feedback whenever they began "hitting" on the target.

The overall results of the experiment are certainly suggestive, but not without a certain amount of complexity. The subjects who took part in the feedback training between their two formal sessions did show evidence of improvement. They seemed to learn from the feedback how to better focus in on the target during the ganzfeld. The only hitch was that the control subjects did not score above chance on either their initial or follow-up sessions. Nor did the training group show any ESP during their first exposure in the ganzfeld. Now this is a bit odd, since much earlier ganzfeld research conducted by Dr. Braud and others had shown that the ganzfeld is, in itself, an ESP-conducive induction procedure. The subjects should have shown at least *some* ESP during all phases of the experiment. This has led Braud to suggest that either his results were due to ESP learning, or that his subjects were somehow aware of the specific results he wanted and expected. They may therefore have tailored their ESP performances to meet them. This is called the "experimenter effect" and is one of the thorniest problems facing parapsychology today.

Despite the uncertainties of Dr. Braud's findings and the capriciousness of Dr. Tart's learning studies, there seems to be more than ample evidence that learning and feedback techniques can play a useful role as one attempts to develop and control ESP. Maybe it isn't the magic wand that will convert the proverbial man on the street into a gifted psychic, but it remains yet another tool parapsychology can use as it explores ways of helping people "learn" the art of being psychic.

APPLYING FEEDBACK TO ESP TESTING

Since feedback is an absurdly simple procedure, no exercises are needed to master the art. Applying feedback to ESP testing does present a few minor problems, though, which you must always keep in mind.

The whole concept of feedback is to give yourself immediate information by which you can determine whether or not you have "hit" the target on which you are focusing or have missed it. Tart argues that you can use learning procedures both in your day-to-day life and as part of your formal self-testing. He maintains, for example, that feedback can be used during the course of your daily life in the same way that dreams can be studied for their possible ESP content. You need merely to take note of any hunches or intuitions that come your way during the day about people you know, future events, what might be happening at a friend's house, and so forth. Be sure then to *act* on your impressions by checking out the accuracy of your hunches and then try to determine what circumstances seem to be associated with genuine ESP messages and how they differ from when your impressions don't pan out. As Dr. Tart suggests:

Start taking detailed records of when you have any kind of intuition or images that you think might be ESP impressions. You should report not only what the context of the image was—what it's about—but what your state was at the time. How did you feel? What led up to it? and so forth. Then go out and check up on the impression. Did this image, vision, or intuition actually come true? Or was it partially true? Or was it false? Start making a collection of your own experiences in detailed notes and then eventually sit down and start reviewing them. Start making discriminations yourself as to what kind of state of mind you were in at the time. Then you can tell that when you feel a certain way when you get an impression, you are right. Teach yourself.

Another way to apply learning theory to your self-development is through card-guessing tests. You can begin rather informally with a deck of ordinary playing cards. Here are some hints Dr. Tart made when I discussed self-testing programs with him:

> Anyone could take a deck of ordinary cards, shuffle it very thoroughly, which means at least eight or ten times, and then pull one card out face down without looking and try to get a psychic impression. What is the card? When you are *sure* you have a psychic impression write it down, then turn the card over right away and see what it is. Are you right or wrong? Are you close to it, even if you're not exactly right? Then, this is important, put the card back in the deck and shuffle the deck very thoroughly again. Try the procedure again. If you don't put the cards back, you'll learn to be a better card player because you'll remember what's been played, but you will fool only yourself by helping your guessing along.

This is, of course, only a very preliminary way of testing your ESP and does entail certain possible complications. The main problem is that this technique invites contamination from the type of sensory cuing I discussed in the chapter on relaxation and card-guessing. If you use the same deck of cards over and over, you might begin to unconsciously memorize which numbers or suits are associated with little nicks or scratches on the backs of the cards. You might eventually score well, but ESP will probably not be what you are learning.

Probably the best way to proceed would be by the use of standard ESP cards. Instructions for using these cards for self-testing have already been given in the chapter on relaxation, so they don't have to be repeated here. There is one catch, though, and it is an important one. ESP card-guessing tests are conducted with either what we call "closed" decks or "open" decks. A closed deck is the type that is commercially available and consists of five sets of five cards printed with each of the various ESP symbols. You cannot use feedback after each trial (by turning the cards over one by one if you are testing yourself for clairvoyance) if you are working with a closed deck. It is too easy to score well towards the end of the run by inadvertently keeping track of how many of each symbol have already appeared. This markedly increases your chances at logically figuring out which symbols are the most likely to come up next. To avoid this problem, you will have to use a deck that consists of an unequal number of each of the five symbols. This obviates the problem of second-guessing. To prepare an open deck for yourself presents no real problem. Merely buy or procure five or so decks of ESP cards, shuffle them all together, and then count off the first twenty-five cards. Now use this deck for your target order, and test yourself accordingly. You can evaluate yourself by using the standard deviation and probability tables presented in the chapter on relaxation.

Since sensory cuing is still a problem under these conditions, you should also buy several small manila envelopes of the sort that coin collectors often use. Place each card in a different envelope before shuffling them, or have a friend do this for you. Remove the cards from their sleeves after each session, reassign them, and shuffle them to prepare your new deck and target order. Do this every time you test yourself or complete a session. This way you will be responding to the envelopes and not to the cards, and will eliminate any possibility of picking up cues from the backs of the cards. Be sure you follow these procedures after each session, though, since you might—after all—learn to respond to creases and nicks on the envelopes if you aren't careful!

You can bypass the problem of sensory cuing altogether if you only test yourself for GESP with the help of a friend willing to act as a sender or agent who can call out when you are right or wrong. But this may become cumbersome if you wish to spend a great deal of time at your psychic development practices.

If you prefer to work with free-response material, you can proceed with the use of pictorial targets such as those I described in the chapter on ESP and mental imagery. Testing yourself with this material can be done in several ways. One way is to divide up your time between training or practice sessions and formal trials. Begin by preparing thirty or so targets, placing each in a separate envelope. Ideally, you should ask a friend to do this for you, or you can cut out the pictures yourself and then have a friend assign them to their folders. Now lie down or sit in a comfortable chair, close your eyes, and wait until the first image pops into your mind. Write down what you just "saw" and then open the envelope and see how well your mental image matches the target. Do this four times and see if you have been able to identify any odd feelings or subjective sensations that seem linked to your success at the task. (In my own case, for instance, I know when I am hitting the target when the image seems to "flash" instead of gradually form in my mind.) After your four practice trials, do an experimental session in which you don't give yourself any feedback. Repeat this entire procedure six times. Then mark down for future reference which target envelopes are related to which of your responses. Randomize both the envelopes and the responses and hand both sets over to a friend. Ask him to rank the targets and the responses along the same lines I suggested in the chapter on ESP and visualization, then compare his ranking to the proper match-ups.

References

Braud, William G. and Wood, Robert. The influence of immediate feedback on free-response GESP performance during ganzfeld stimulation. *Journal* of the American Society for Psychical Research, 1977, *71*, 409–28.

Stanford, Rex. The application of learning theory to ESP performance: a review of Dr. C. T. Tart's monograph. *Journal* of the American Society for Psychical Research, 1977, *71*, 55–80.

Targ, Russell and Hurt, David B. Learning clairvoyance and perception with an extrasensory perception teaching machine. *Parapsycholgoy Review*, 1972, 3, *4*, 9–11.

Tart, Charles T. *The Application of Learning Theory to Extrasensory Perception.* New York: Parapsychology Foundation, 1975.

Tart, Charles T. *Learning to Use Extrasensory Perception.* Chicago: University of Chicago Press, 1976.

Tart, Charles T. Towards humanistic experimentation in parapsychology: a reply to Dr. Stanford's review. *Journal* of the American Society for Psychical Research, 1977, *71*, 81–102.

Tart, Charles T.; Palmer, John; and Redington, Dana. Effects of immediate feedback on ESP performance: a second study. *Journal* of the American Society for Psychical Research, 1979, *73*, 151–66.

Tart, Charles T.; Palmer, John; Redington, D. J. Effects of immediate feedback on ESP performance over short time periods. *Journal* of the American Society for Psychical Research, 1979, *73*, 291–302.

conclusion: the truth about psychic development courses

Browsed about any paperback bookstores lately? If you're the type who likes to linger around airport bookstalls or enjoys glancing through the latest gothic novels at your local liquor store, you've probably noted the surge of books now available on "learning" or "developing" ESP. Books such as *Making ESP Work for You, Seven Steps to Psychic Power, Guidebook to Psychic Healing,* and others not only populate the mass book market, they even seem to be multiplying! In this era of self-discovery—where such terms as "vibrations," "awareness," "experience," *ad infinitum* and *ad nauseum* are becoming part of everyday language—people all over the country are taking an interest in developing their psychic abilities. Although it is true that several parapsychologists have discovered the existence of semireliable psi-conducive states of mind, few of them—with the notable exception of Dr. Milan Ryzl, whose work was analyzed in a previous chapter—have actually developed home "do-it-yourself" ESP programs. Nonetheless, it is rather surprising how many courses promising to help you develop ESP powers are now being commercially offered by home study course marketeers and by so-called "mind dynamics" organizations. The proliferation of these courses obviously reflects the inherent marketability of ESP. They are being offered because many people today seem eager to develop abilities ranging from simple ESP to astral projection! The rise of interest in psychic development is actually one of pop culture's most intriguing phenomena.

But *can* you develop ESP? Do books and courses of the type mentioned above really work? And what about commercially available "mind dynamics" courses? Can a fee of about $300.00, which most of these programs cost, guarantee you psychic powers for the taking?

In other words, is systematic "psychic development" a reality? Or is it another in a long series of consumer rip-offs which the public should be warned against? While most parapsychologists tend to shy away from commenting on such issues, the popularity of these training procedures and courses have irked a number of researchers enough so that they have decided to look into their possible efficacy. The research conducted by this handful of trained and qualified parapsychologists in the United States has begun to shed some light on the marketability of ESP.

The Silva Mind Control method is perhaps the most popular mind dynamics course readily available in the United States. It has graduated thousands of clients and its popularity is rivaled only by *est*. The popularity of the Silva method is best illustrated by the fact that when its founder, José Silva, wrote a book on his method, it quickly became a selection of the *Psychology Today* Book Club.

José Silva was born in Laredo, Texas, in 1914. He began his career as a part-time college teacher, during which time he became interested in hypnosis and how it could be used as an educational aid. He found that his private students seemed capable of remembering facts and figures better when hypnotized than when attempting to learn their lessons in a normal and alert state. Silva soon abandoned hypnosis, however, and began exploring alternate methods of disciplining the mind so that it would be capable of better intellectual and academic performance. This led him to the study of meditation, ESP, and other "human potentials" exercises. He eventually burst onto the public scene sometime in the late 1960s with his "Silva Mind Control Method," which he had apparently developed back in the 1950s. This training procedure, which costs a few hundred dollars to undergo, consists of teaching clients to meditate, remain mentally alert while simultaneously relaxing the body, to induce this state at will, and learn to deliberately produce and retain mental images. The ultimate goal of the procedure is to teach the client to reach and enter this level of alert relaxation at will—any time and any place. The entire training program takes only a couple of days to complete and is conducted at Silva offices around the country.

Although Silva stresses that his techniques are not truly akin to formal hypnosis, there can be little doubt but that this method is very much a form of autohypnosis. In fact, some of his techniques are very like those taught by commercial mail order courses and institutions that teach autohypnosis.

And just how and why do his course and exercises work?

Silva himself has offered an explanation for the success of his training program by drawing on some recent findings from the field of psychophysiology. Psychologists have long known that the brain produces different electrical rhythms when it enters into different states of activity. The pulsations can be easily recorded and monitored when a person is hooked to an electroencephalograph. When you or I are alert and dealing with our day to day problems and concerns, our minds usually produce what are called "beta waves." These are relatively fast electrical impulses emitted by the brain when it is, for instance, solving a mathematical problem or engaged in an intellectual discussion. When we relax and try to clear our minds, such as one does when attempting to meditate, our minds also become more quiescent and produce slower waves. These pulsations, called "alpha waves," typically occur when one is relaxing and trying to remain mentally and physically calm. As mentioned above, psychologists have found that meditators often produce an abundance of "alpha waves" when deep in their inner worlds. Silva believes that "going into alpha" is the key to developing greater intellectual capabilities and also is the key to psychic powers.

This isn't the time or place to discuss the validity of Silva's claims about the nature of alpha brainwaves. Suffice it to say that psychophysiology is a vastly complex field and that the nature of alpha brain waves are much more complex than Silva would have you believe. They can be produced under all sorts of conditions. It is also rather curious that Silva's techniques teach the client to "enter alpha" (as he terms it),relax, and visualize. Psychophysiologists learned years ago that the brain will usually stop producing alpha waves when an experimental subject is asked to hold a mental picture in his mind! But for now we will be more concerned with the psychic aspects of the Silva procedures.

Although emphasizing that it is a psychological technique, proponents of the Silva techniques promise that they can help you develop ESP—from clairvoyance to aura reading—and publicly advertise that no one has yet failed to do so!

According to the introduction to *The Silva Mind Control Method*, the Silva method is the "first method in history that can train anybody to use ESP." The introduction goes on to claim that Silva himself, working in Texas in the early 1950s, was able to train all of the thirty-nine children with whom he initially worked, as he developed his techniques, to develop and control their ESP talents.

Silva himself has forthrightly stated that his rather simple techniques can help just about anyone tap inner ESP abilities. In the chapter of his book on "You *Can* Practice ESP," he is more than generous with such claims. He states, for instance, that his method trains people to "perform psychically with real life in ways so exciting that they experience a sort of spiritual 'high' so exquisitely intense that their lives are never quite the same again." This is quite a claim in light of the fact that, according to Silva, this occurs "at the end of forty hours of instruction and exercises."

These exercises, like the program itself, stress simplicity. The student is instructed to visualize his home, project himself to it, and explore it mentally by entering into its walls, etc. He is then instructed to enter into other types of physical objects and explore their inner structures. Finally, he procedes to penetrate organic objects, such as trees and animals, and examines the inner biology of living matter. This leads him to the final stages of the program, during which he is asked to enter into the body of a person and carry out the same procedure. It also helps, according to Silva, if one makes contact with a "counselor"—some sort of higher personality within the self—who can help guide the student as he carries out this phase of the training. The ultimate goal of the program is to teach students how to scan the bodies of people located even miles away, clairvoyantly diagnose any medical conditions existing there. In fact, at the end of the Silva course, all students take an ESP test during which they attempt two such diagnoses. A Silva examiner provides the client with the names of two people who are not present. He is then told to make a psychic diagnosis of each of the patients. Graduation from the course is contingent on success. But the question still remains whether Silva Mind Control claims can be backed up by empirical data.

Some anecdotal evidence that this method does work has recently been published by Dr. Stephen A. Appelbaum, formerly a psychoanalyst with the Kansas-based Menninger Foundation, who was specifically requested by the Foundation to study and report on human potential trainings and therapies. In his report, a massive but entertaining volume entitled *Out in Inner Space*, Appelbaum spends a generous portion of his time discussing mind control courses. The psychiatrist himself underwent the

Silva program and was rather surprised by his own success at "becoming psychic," and was more than intrigued by his newfound ability to successfully diagnose people at a distance.

For one diagnosis, he was given only the name of the person he was asked to examine, along with her age, sex, and address. His impressions of the patient were as follows:

> Arms outstretched, she is black, I see a curved thing from the left hip to the right armpit, now the lower back, the left side, above the buttock, where the kidney is, tilted left higher than right at the hip, she's crippled, the idea of falling, experience of falling. The arms have receded in my mind, the tilted pelvis and hip dominate the picture. I feel sorry for her. She is in severe distress, a cripple, muscles are affected. I can't see her head. I can't make much of her head, that seems not important.

Appelbaum later learned that his subject had multiple sclerosis. Most of his impressions were correct except for the fact that the woman wasn't black.

He was similarly successful when attempting six other readings. When given the name of a young woman, for instance, he psychically "saw" her lying in a hospital bed with straps holding her feet. Her condition reminded him of paralysis. He even told his examiner that he felt himself "sitting in a chair like a paraplegic," and saw the girl clenching her fists. This wasn't a bad diagnosis at all considering the fact that the reading was being given for a girl who had just been operated on for polio. Appelbaum could not, unfortunately, discover whether the girl was actually in the hospital at the time of the reading.

It is interesting that Appelbaum took the Silva course as part of a project and survey he was conducting into "new age" psychology for the Menninger Foundation. He wasn't an ESP buff by any means, nor was he interested in the Silva course for any reason other than professional curiosity. In this regard you might say he was a rather atypical Silva client. Yet even under these circumstances, Appelbaum was apparently able to demonstrate ESP after taking the training seminar.

Testimony of this sort is available by the handful. But this type of anecdotal evidence does have its weaknesses. For one thing, Appelbaum never initially tested himself to see if he had any psychic abilities *before* taking the Silva course, so we really can't say that the Silva method unequivocally helped him develop ESP. He may have had it all along. There is also the problem that, in most cases, the person supplying the name of the patient to the student is also the examiner who guides him through the diagnoses. The examiner may, then, often "clue" the student by subtle innuendos or leading questions about what he should be reporting. Appelbaum is keenly aware of this problem, and notes in his book that "there is opportunity for the orientologist to reinforce diagnostic inferences that could have come about through chance and thus in effect guide the psychic toward the correct information."

For example, let's say that I am taking the Silva examination and am reading for someone with lower back pain. I might begin by making some innocuous statement such as "I see the patient has a back problem." Now this is a pretty general remark since many people suffer from back pain of one sort or another. But my examiner could ask, quite innocently, "Oh, can you tell me more about that?" Such a question might clue me to the fact that I am on the right track. So I might say, "It's a problem near the shoulders." The examiner could drop his face a bit and say, "No, that's not quite it. Try to see it clearer." Inadvertently following the clue, I might then say, "Oh, yes. It's in the lower back—it's a problem with lower back pain!" The examiner would then congratulate me on my success and I would leave the Silva program convinced that I had diagnosed the problem all by myself!

Despite such problems, the fact remains that *some* Silva graduates do tend to perform well on conventional ESP tests. I can vouch for this from personal experience. In 1975 I met an attractive young actress, Claudia Adams, who was a recent Silva graduate. She had even been invited to become a Silva instructor, but had declined in order to pursue her career. I was conducting some ganzfeld ESP tests at the time and recruited her as one of my subjects. I didn't know quite what I was in for.

I discovered that I had found an extraordinary ESP talent during my first experiment with her.

The experiments I was conducting at the time were being run using a procedure similar to the one worked out at the Maimonides Medical Center. They were being conducted at the U.C.L.A. Neuropsychiatric Institute, where a friendly faculty member had lent me her lab, which luckily included an isolation booth. We were using viewmaster reels as the ESP targets. I was acting as the chief experimenter for the project, while an assistant of mine, Chris Shepherd, acted as agent. Because of space limitations we couldn't use a two-room setup for the sessions, so I had stationed Chris in a position next to the booth and out of my sight, while from a position in front of the booth I recorded the subject's mentation over an intercom.

The experimental reel for the test I ran with Claudia, who began as only one of some forty subjects I was testing, was titled "The American

Indian." No sooner had my assistant begun viewing the reel than Claudia reported from the booth that she saw, "Natives ... native people. I see a bunch of naked people. Also like a mother with a child in her arms." This was an accurate description of the scene my assistant was viewing at the time. At that moment, however, Chris decided to click the viewmaster to the next scene on the reel which depicted an aerial view of a large expanse of forestland. Two dirt roads met within the forest. At the very time Chris began looking at this scene, Claudia reported from the booth that she saw "a forest with a lot of trees ... all the trees seem to be in a line," and then went on to describe the forest in greater detail. Then Chris clicked the viewmaster again to yet a third scene. This one pictured two Indians paddling a canoe. Claudia's mental imagery flowed right along with the change of scene. No sooner had Chris clicked to this scene than Caludia piped up, "A sailboat ... no sail, it's a plain boat. It's rocking up and down on the waves."

Claudia's performance was one of the most outstanding demonstrations of ESP I have ever witnessed—in the laboratory or out! My assistant was literally stunned by her success, since he had been able to hear what Claudia was reporting over the intercom from his position by the booth. This was the first time he had ever witnessed a direct display of ESP.

But our amazement didn't end there. When I transcribed Claudia's tape I discovered that, even *before* Chris had begun viewing the reel of slides, she had already tuned into it. Claudia had been in the ganzfeld for several minutes before Chris even opened the blank envelope containing the slides. During this time she gave us a beautiful description of the forest scene with the crossed roads. Just a few minutes after the session began, Claudia had reported that she saw "trees, looking down on trees, a lot; it's a forestland or what. Airplane overlooking forestland." Moments later she went on to report that "a road comes into another road; it's not a cross section, just one road coming into another road. A dirt road." So while we had been primarily interested in testing Claudia's telepathic talents, our subject had done us one better by giving us a stunning display of clairvoyance! And this is, after all, the type of ESP the Silva people claim to teach.

I was so impressed by the outcome of this test that I decided to conduct a whole series of experiments with Claudia, who turned out to be an ideal subject.

Her willingness to cooperate in controlled tests was unfailing, and after several pilot studies, I carried out a crucial series of ten tests with Claudia at the U.C.L. A. Neuropsychiatric Institute. I placed Claudia in my sound-attenuated booth for each of these sessions, placed halved ping-pong balls over her eyes, and had her stare into a dim red light. I did not use any auditory ganzfeld. The chamber was sealed after I gave her instructions to report over an intercom any mental images which might come to mind for periods of only ten to fifteen minutes. During that time, I randomly chose a viewmaster slide from a target pool of forty and looked at it continuously. Claudia's job, of course, was to try to generate mental images which matched what I was seeing. And sometimes she was remarkably apt at doing it.

When, for instance, I was looking at a series of slides depicting California missions, Claudia reported, "Steps. There's a thing like a California type of house, lots of greenery around, and there's a chimney ... it's either gray ... if it's a natural thing it's gray ... it is almost alabaster white." And when I was looking at a scene from Disneyland's *Frontierland* depicting a train rushing through a series of tall cacti, she responded, "There's a highway, going down like a highway ... There's a lot of telephone poles. I think [I am] in a car, but I think it could be a train. And it's going, like passing, telephone poles ..." My favorite response, though, came when I was viewing scenes from a Walt Disney cartoon. As I actually viewed them my subject reported back to me over the intercom, "... cartoon things, but I get the feeling of it being cartoonery on the one hand and on the other I get the feeling of it being a scene. I almost get the feeling like of a Walt Disney 'Song of the South' sort of thing ..."

These experiments were not without their humorous side. When I was viewing a picture of Batman and Robin in their bat cave, taken from the Adam West series of some years back, Claudia reported to me, "I see a crevice, it could be a rock formation. It's like looking through a long cylinder or a pipe stuck into a hole and a rock of some sort ... I see a *robin* with a very red front and its head is up."

You can well imagine how impressive and awesome it is to hear someone reporting these scenes so accurately from a sealed booth while you are actually looking at them!

It is impossible, however, to determine what role Claudia's training in the Silva Mind Control course played in her outstanding successes during my ESP tests with her. Since I did not know Claudia before she took the course, I have no way of knowing whether she possessed ESP ability before she took the training seminar. I pointed out in Chapters 2 and 3 that visualization techniques do seem to be a road to ESP. Claudia, an actress by profession, is gifted with the capability to "drop out" of her normal personality and transcend it. Her powers of mental visualization, which she learned as part of her training on the stage, is also formidable. These abilities, in themselves, may be positively related to ESP abilities. So it could well be that Claudia just happens to be an outstanding ESP subject apart from her Silva training. It is also quite possible that it was the ganzfeld technique itself that helped mitigate her success. As I also pointed out in Chapter 2, the ganzfeld is a powerful technique which seems to help many people tap their ESP potentials. It is therefore a moot point whether it was the Silva training or the ganzfeld setting that was the crucial factor in Claudia's ability to demonstrate ESP during our work together.

However, I should point out that there are several factors which led me to believe that the ganzfeld setting could not have been solely responsible for Claudia's performance. First of all, I did not use any auditory ganzfeld during my work with her. I merely had Claudia undergo visual ganzfeld stimulation. Now this abbreviated procedure actually undermines the effect of the ganzfeld for most people. Psychologists have learned that many volunteers only report strong mental imagery when both visual *and* auditory stimulation are combined. Visual stimulation alone usually doesn't do the trick. There is also evidence that experimental ESP subjects only do well in the ganzfeld after they have been exposed to its effects for a lengthy period of time. Both Charles Honorton, when he was at the Maimonides Medical Center, and Dr. Carl Sargent at Cambridge University have determined that their subjects perform best during ganzfeld sessions lasting up to 40 minutes. Yet I found that Claudia did her best when I utilized sessions of only about 10 minutes. (Later in 1975 I tried testing other subjects with short duration ganzfeld sessions while conducting some research under Chuck Honorton's direction at the Maimonides lab. I had little success with it.) So Claudia's performance stands in striking contrast to the way most people respond to the ganzfeld.

So my work with Claudia proved to me that, at least *prima facie*, parapsychologists should be taking the claims made by mind control groups seriously. Claudia herself firmly believes that the Silva method appreciably enhanced her psychic talents and urged me repeatedly to test other Silva graduates. She never considered herself as especially talented, and provided me with many impressive stories of ESP demonstrations she had seen other Silva graduates perform. I might also add that a colleague of mine once told me that the two most extraordinary psychics he ever tested claimed to have developed their talents through these courses.

Despite this evidence, though, specific *tests* of Silva Mind Control claims have not fared too well.

One such test was reported a few years ago by three veteran New York parapsychologists. Dr. Bob Brier of C. W. Post College, Dr. Gertrude

Schmeidler of City College, and Dr. Barry Savits of St. Mary's Hospital in New York were intrigued enough with Silva claims to design and conduct a series of three experiments using an experimental procedure used by the Silva people themselves. These tests are more revealing than my work with Claudia since it tested the Silva claims at face value. Their report, which was published in the July 1975 issue of the *Journal* of the American Society for Psychical Research, is an eye-opener.

Ten Silva graduates were recruited for the first experiment and were tested at their homes. Each subject was asked to give medical readings for five of Dr. Savits' patients. The subjects were mailed the names of the patients, so the "readings" were not made in the presence of anyone who had any information on the patients' medical histories. The subjects were also provided with a set of anatomy charts, one each for every patient, on which they could circle any areas they diagnosed as "trouble spots." All these data were subsequently mailed to Dr. Schmeidler at City College. She, in turn, randomized them and sent them to Savits. His job was to figure out which reading was meant for which of his patients. Only five of the graduates completed the project.

If the Silva graduates had given accurate diagnoses, Savits should have had no problem making the matches. However, he found the readings so inaccurate that he was unable to correctly determine which "reading" was meant for which patient.

For their second experiment, the three New York investigators recruited five students who had graduated from the Silva course that very day. This experiment was implemented to offset the criticism that their initial subjects, some of whom had taken the seminar as far back as two years prior, might not represent a fair sampling of what Silva graduates could really do. According to Silva claims, then, these five students should have been in top form for the test. The same design was used as in the first experiment. Nonetheless, these subjects did as poorly as the first group, though one of them did tend to show a cursory level of accuracy.

The third test was conducted directly in collaboration with the Silva Mind Control organization. In order to implement this last and most ambitious test, both Bob Brier and a friend of his, Barbara Benton, actually took the Silva course in New York. On the day they graduated the program they tested several of their fellow students by asking them to diagnose the ills of patients whose names had been provided by Dr. Savits. They then visited two other mind control classes over the next few weeks and tested several more subjects upon the day of their graduation and

146

when their ESP abilities should have been at their peak. There was, however, an important hitch to this experiment. Sometimes the experimenters knew *in advance* exactly what was wrong with the patients whose names had been supplied by Savits. The other examinations were done blindly. (That is, neither Brier nor Benton had any idea what was wrong with the people whose names they had been given.)

The results of this test accorded quite nicely with the "sensory cuing" theory. The Silva graduates who were tested under tight double-blind conditions scored miserably. However, those graduates who had been tested by Brier and Benton under non-blind conditions (i.e., when the experimenters themselves knew what was wrong with the patients) performed remarkably well!

Dr. Brier and Dr. Schmeidler admit, in light of these results, that Silva graduates may be only capable of ESP when tested for telepathy, which could explain why they only did well when Brier and Benton knew what was wrong with the target patients. However they tend to reject this idea in their report. They prefer to believe that Brier and Benton may have accidently cued their subjects and guided their responses in a most subtle way.*

As they point out in their report, the Silva people give their examiners fairly stringent instructions on how to test their graduating students for ESP. These instructions encourage them to clue their clients about the diagnoses they are expected to give. When the client says something that is clearly incorrect, the examiner is told to suggest the student look elsewhere and not respond directly in the negative. By following this procedure, the examiner may consciously or unconsciously guide the client into making the correct diagnosis.

Of course, the Brier/Benton finding isn't new, since other critics of the Silva method make similar charges.

By using such inadvertent cuing it isn't surprising that the Silva people procure good ESP results most of the time. Dr. Stephen Applebaum made a similar discovery during his Menninger work, although he didn't feel that "cuing" could explain all the results he witnessed.

On the basis of these tests, Brier and his co-workers have concluded that there is little evidence that the Silva course helps people

---

*Many parapsychologists have found that experimental ESP subjects do equally well on both telepathy and clairvoyance tests. This discovery was initially made by J. B. Rhine during his early Duke years in the 1930s, and has been replicated many times since by other research workers.

develop psychic abilities. But they do not disdain the obvious need for more research on the subject.

And more research has indeed been done. A further investigation into Silva claims was carried out by Alan Vaughan, at the time a researcher in San Francisco, shortly after Brier's project was completed. The results of his research were reported at the 16th Annual Convention of the Parapsychological Association held in August 1973 in Charlottesville, Virginia. Vaughan tested 21 Silva graduates from the Bay area using a design similar to Brier's. Each was asked to make a medical diagnosis for a person whose name was provided by the experimenter. But the results were disheartening. Although a total of 21 readings were done, only one subject made a single correct diagnostic statement.

Test results such as these tend to put Silva claims in doubt. And the failure of Silva graduates to show psychic ability when tested under controlled conditions makes the claims made by similar mind dynamics courses equally suspect. *Est* (Erhard Training Seminars), a mind-control procedure developed by Werner Erhard in San Francisco, even tests its students upon graduation with the same clairvoyant diagnosis task that the Silva people use.

To date, then, parapsychologists have had mixed reactions to mind-control courses and their claims. Dr. Rex Stanford, a Texas parapsychologist now at St. John's University in New York, has suggested that some people who graduate from these seminars may develop "delusional" thinking about possessing psychic powers:

> As a parapsychologist I have come into contact with many persons who have graduated from such courses. Many retain reasonable, objective perspectives on what happened to them in the course and on what had been the long-term result. On the other hand, a small proportion of those who have undergone such training come out of the course believing themselves endowed with almost unlimited capacities to manipulate other people by psychic means and they seem fixated on these possibilities. Some mind-control type courses include the claim that graduates cannot only use ESP but can influence others mentally and physically and can even influence inanimate matter. It is my considered opinion that some such courses encourage and support bizarre and unrealistic ideation in the student and that this might seriously exacerbate the psychological instability of persons who enter the course in an intiially unstable state of mind.

He has also pointed out that such organizations may be misguiding the general public. "Usually such organizations create the appearance that they are scientifically oriented benefactors of the future 'evolution' of this planet," writes Stanford. But, he adds, they do so by using "language which appears scientific to the layman, but which is really pseudoscientific." Stanford goes on to say that such courses typically talk about the mind and the brain waves it produces in such a naive way that their teachings "should provide suitable bedtime fairy-tale material for the psychophysiologist." Stanford has pointed out a gross fallacy made by mind control proponents who claim that there exists a relationship between ESP and alpha brain waves, which is a key teaching of Silva adherents. He correctly points out that many parapsychologists, including himself, have tested their subjects for ESP while their brain waves were being monitored. So far they have found no consistent relationship between ESP and alpha brain waves.

In conclusion, Stanford feels that mind control courses potentially pose at least one further threat. He feels that graduates of these programs might dissuade their friends and relatives from seeking proper medical examinations when ill by providing more convenient (and much cheaper) "psychic diagnoses" which would probably be extremely inaccurate. Stanford also indicates that several mind control courses teach their clients to develop alleged healing powers and that mind control graduates might try to "treat" their acquaintances and thus discourage them from getting proper medical treatment.

Stanford's views represent an extreme position within the parapsychological community. They are certainly not shared by all ESP researchers. Dr. Arthur Hastings, a parapsychologist from northern California, has recently stated that parapsychologists may have a lot to learn from mind control courses. As he reported to the 1979 convention of the Parapsychological Association held at St. Mary's College in Moraga, California, these techniques are designed to help people make contact with the subjective workings of the mind. These methods may thus help us to tap inner psychic resources. Hastings is now urging parapsychologists to recruit mind control course graduates for proper parapsychological testing. "Inasmuch as the [se] techniques are reported to produce psi," Hastings stated during his talk, "they deserve investigation by serious researchers." He went on to say that the graduates of such programs may provide the parapsychological community with a pool of potentially talented subjects for ESP tests.

However, the results of the carefully conducted tests by Brier and Alan Vaughan may well dissuade researchers from seriously studying mind control course techniques.

But what of other "self-help" ESP courses? Are they as open to question as the Silva method?

A very different approach to the value of psychic development techniques is currently being undertaken by Dr. Robert Morris, who was until recently a parapsychologist at the University of California, Irvine. Morris has long been interested in comparing and evaluating "do-it-yourself" techniques reputedly proficient in helping people develop psychic abilities. To date he has discovered that most popular books on the subject of psychic self-help incorporate very similar teachings and methods. Dr. Morris was actively engaged in experimentally testing out some of these techniques in his laboratory until his move in 1980 to Syracuse University in New York.

Morris began his project in 1975 with the help of several of his parapsychology students when he was still teaching at the University of California at Santa Barbara. The students were asked to find psychic development manuals of the type sold at newsstands or liquor store book racks, and outline their contents. Morris himself collated all these training procedures into a systematic catalog over a several month period and reported on his work in 1976 at a convention of the Parapsychological Association held at the University of Utrecht in Holland. All in all, seventy-four books written by a total of fifty-seven authors were surveyed. From these books Morris was able to extract the following general guidelines recommended for psychic development:

1. The subject should be in good health.
2. While no specific diet was recommended, meatless diets were suggested during certain phases of development.
3. The student was to adopt a positive, receptive attitude about psychic development, and remain confident that psychic powers *would* result from the course.
4. There was a tendency for these books to encourage their readers to adopt religious or quasireligious belief systems.
5. One should learn to become more attentive to dreams, hunches, etc.
6. Psychic training should be practiced once a day or so, through the practice of progressive muscular relaxation.
7. Concentration should be focused inwardly.
8. Meditation was recommended.
9. The student should learn how to eject extraneous thoughts from his mind in order to keep it as clear as possible for the reception of psychic information.

At this point the various manuals Morris and his staff surveyed taught a diversity of approaches toward actually learning to use ESP and psychokinesis (or "mind over matter"). As Morris reported in his presentation to the convention:

> At this point the advice became much more varied. Several of the books suggested allowing the body and mind-clearing procedures to lead directly into a dreamlike state or a period of quiet concentration, during which psychic impressions would gradually come forth. Others advocated the use of some specific sort of imagery to facilitate the psi process, such as imagining a beam of light or a long tube extending out towards the target and moving "energy" along that tube. Agents and receivers were advised to visualize each other. For PK, the target (or any other goal) should be visualized repeatedly. Many authors advocated the frequent visualization of light and other "energy" flowing through the body.

Dr. Morris was impressed with how consistent some of this advice appears to be with what parapsychologists have discovered through systematic experimentation. As was pointed out in earlier chapters, considerable experimental evidence exists which indicates that belief in ESP, internal focusing techniques, the ability to control mental imagery, and relaxation are all positively related to the development of ESP ability. So the main teachings of most "do-it-yourself" ESP manuals seem to be basically on the right track. But much of this same advice, according to Morris, enters into domains parapsychologists have so far failed to explore experimentally.

"Much of this advice is consistent with research findings," stated Morris during his presentation to the Parapsychological Association. "The facilitating effects of confidence, positive attitude, progressive relaxation, and 'mind-clearing' techniques have been frequent topics of research." But, he adds, "very little developmental work with selected individuals has been done in recent years under controlled circumstances to examine the growth of psi ability upon application of these procedures. And finally, almost no research has attempted to combine the factors discussed above to maximize their effectiveness."

So far, Morris has designed two experiments specifically developed to test the techniques suggested in these books. The first was conducted while he was still at the University of California, Santa Barbara. Eighteen students from U.C.S.B. were tested after being trained in procedures which Morris had culled from psychic self-help manuals of the type mentioned above. He and several of his students acted as experimenters. Each subject was taken to an experimental room at the university and was trained first in progressive muscular relaxation. They were then asked to pay attention to their mental imagery for exactly four minutes. The subject reported his mental imagery to the experimenter, who kept a log on them. During this time, the experimenter had a "sender" (stationed in another room in the building) concentrate on a picture slide. The subject was instructed to try to pick up what the sender was viewing by incorporating it into his mental imagery. After the four-minute period, the experimenter read back to the subject a list of the images he had reported and asked him to draw pictures of them. Each of the subjects was tested four times over a several week period, and told to practice a similar exercise at home. None of the subjects showed any ESP ability at all during any portion of the experiment.

Morris's second experiment fared much better. This was a study to see if psychokinetic (PK) abilities could be enhanced through self-development techniques. For this experiment, Morris compared two methods taught in psychic development manuals which claim to help anyone develop such powers. One of these techniques, which Morris labeled as "process oriented," teaches the student to imagine "psychic energy" flowing to the person or object he wishes to affect, and more or less actively interact with the target. The other technique teaches one to enter into a passive frame of mind and "visualize" and hold in mind the final outcome of whatever the student is trying to achieve. Morris has called this technique the "goal oriented" method.

The subjects, who were once again mostly U.C.S.B. students, were trained in these procedures and then tested on an apparatus often used by parapsychologists for PK testing. The apparatus consists basically of a circle of lights. When the device is activated, the lights will blink sequentially in a random order, either tending to move in clockwise or counterclockwise motion around the circle. The subject's task is to bias the lights so that they move in one direction more consistently than in the other. In order to achieve this goal, the subject must use his PK abilities to interfere with the internal workings of the highly complex apparatus.

Morris's results were quite interesting. The process-oriented technique seemed to have no effect on the apparatus. However, the students who used the "goal oriented" technique did, in fact, seem able to demonstrate PK during the test! Thus, believes Morris, this psychic strategy may indeed be a valid way for people to develop PK abilities. This may very well be true, for this same experiment has just recently been partially replicated by two researchers at Yale University.

In conclusion, the tone of this chapter may seem somewhat pessimistic since parapsychological research has not validated the widely commercialized claims that psychic development courses and manuals can help develop psychic abilities. Nor has this research established any truly reliable techniques that can offer the potential student an instant key to psychic powers. On the other hand, there does seem to be some evidence, scattered though it may be, that *some* of these commercial techniques may work for *some* people *some* of the time. They may even work consistently for a handful of individuals. But little more can be claimed for them.

I don't mean to imply that students of the human potentials movement should stop reading self-help manuals or shy away from commercial mind control courses. Such sources of training may well have heuristic value for the inquirer. But we should be wary of exaggerated claims. While psychic development appears indeed to be a potential we all possess, it may be a torturous road to travel—or at least one cluttered with more obstacles than most psychic self-help groups and books would like us to believe.

In conclusion, please remember that *all* worthwhile accomplishments in life require application and hard work. If you believe, as I do, that the rewards to be reaped from developing our psychic potentials are worthwhile enough to warrant a great deal of effort, you have already won half the battle.

References

Appelbaum, Stephen A. *Out in Inner Space*. Garden City: Anchor/Doubleday, 1979.

Brier, Bob, Schmeidler, Gertrude, and Savits, Barry. Three experiments in clairvoyant diagnosis with Silva Mind Control graduates. *Journal* of the American Society for Psychical Research, 1975, *69*, 263–72.

Morris, Robert and Baily, Kathleen. A preliminary exploration of some techniques reputed to improve free-response ESP. In *Research in Parapsychology-1978*, Metuchen, New Jersey: Scarecrow Press, 1979.

Morris, Robert, Nanko, Michael, and Phillips, David. Intentional observer influence upon measurements for a quantum mechanical system: a comparison of two imagery strategies. In *Research in Parapsychology-1978*. Metuchen, New Jersey: Scarecrow Press, 1979.

Silva, José. *The Silva Mind Control Method*. New York: Simon & Schuster, 1977.

Stanford, Rex. Scientific, ethical and clinical problems in the "training" of psi ability. In *Surveys in Parapsychology* edited by Rhea A. White. Metuchen, New Jersey: Scarecrow Press, 1976.

Vaughan, Alan. Investigation of Silva Mind Control claims. In *Research in Parapsychology-1973*. Metuchen, New Jersey: Scarecrow Press, 1974.

appendix I: judging free-response material

Determining whether you have correctly called down through a pack of standard ESP cards is a relatively easy matter. You merely have to count up your hits and misses, and then apply some simple mathematics to your data. It is much more difficult to evaluate free-response material, such as art prints or magazine photographs. Here you must decide how closely your imagery or impressions match the picture or part of the picture, or you must use your impressions to pick the target from a pool of five or six prints placed before you by an experimenter.

ESP works through primary process thinking, which is rich in symbolism, distortion, and metaphor. If the ESP target is a picture of a mermaid swimming near a ship, you probably won't receive a literal impression of the scene. You may receive impressions just relating to the mermaid, or just to the ship, or you may only get the vague feeling that the whole scene revolves around water. If you look back to what I wrote about my experiments with Claudia Adams, you'll get a good idea of the many ways ESP information is distorted before it makes its way into the waking mind. Sometimes her impressions were very literal, while at other moments they were symbolized or fragmented. Anyone who has worked with free-response material has run into just these sorts of problems.

Because of the distortion which occurs when ESP information is processed, it sometimes takes a great deal of familiarity with how ESP operates in order to judge free-response material astutely. All of us actively involved in parapsychology have sometimes watched our subjects perform beautifully on a free-response test, but then fail to recognize how well they did because they expected to receive a literal impression of the target. My favorite story came from a colleague who was running a ganzfeld session in which magazine photographs were used as the target material. The subject described a tiger pacing restlessly in a cage. The actual target turned out to be a prison inmate looking out from his cell. Believe it or not, the subject simply couldn't see the tie-in between the target and her psychic impressions. This is why Dr. Milan Ryzl spends so much time educating his subjects about the distortions that so often disrupt the clarity of the ESP channel.

If you wish to use free-response target material as you test yourself, you should be thoroughly familiar with the many distortions to which your ESP impressions may be prone. Knowing these sources of error will help you to hone your sixth sense as you practice.

A real pioneer in the study of how ESP imagery enters the conscious mind was René Warcollier, a French engineer who was the president of the Institute Metapsychique in Paris from 1951 until his death in 1962. He was a gifted psychic as well as an innovative experimenter and conducted a great deal of research on the telepathic transmission of pictorial material. In his book *Mind to Mind** he outlined the many ways that ESP emerges from the unconscious in distorted form:

1. If geometric figures or drawings are used, the various components may be received independently and in disjointed fashion. For example, a circle inside a square may be received as a circle *and* a square.
2. A picture may not be received at the precise time it is sent, but only minutes or even hours later.
3. The target may be received in symbolic rather than literal form.
4. All the component parts of the target picture may be received independently so that the content of the picture is all there but not the overall meaning.
5. Likewise, separate components of the picture may be amalgamated.
6. The target may be received via a global impression, while none of the actual specifics of the target will be reproduced.

*New York: Creative Age Press, 1948.

7. Motion will sometimes be added to a static target.
8. The background of the target may be received with equal attention as the central theme or figure.

Parapsychologists are keenly aware of how difficult it can be to judge the ESP component of a subject's response when it is obscured by such distortions. So many researchers who have focused on free-response testing educate their subjects about the problems they will face at first when trying to analyze their impressions—and especially when they must pick out the target sent to them during a particular experiment from a pool of control pictures. It has therefore become customary to provide inexperienced subjects with guidelines by which to judge their impressions, especially when taking part in a formal experiment.

The following set of instructions offers excellent advice on how to evaluate free-response material. These instructions have been slightly revised from those used by Dr. Rex Stanford at St. John's University, who has in the past investigated the relationship between ESP and relaxation as well as the ganzfeld setting. You might want to read them over when you judge your own target responses:

In front of you are five pictures. One of these is the target picture, which was randomly chosen for this session, while the other four are control pictures selected from the same group of pictures as was the target. Your target for the experiment is located randomly among the other four pictures. Therefore, it could be any one of these five pictures. Do not assume that it is supposed to be in any special position among the five. We will check up afterwards to see which is the actual target.

In making your ratings, you should look for the following kinds of correspondences:

1. The most striking kind of correspondence, of course, is a *direct correspondence*. For example, the target might be a bird and you actually experienced a bird during the test.
2. The correspondence may also be a *symbolic correspondence*; i.e., what you experienced during the test symbolizes the picture or the picture seems symbolic of what you experienced. For example, if you experienced a cross during the test, this may indicate that the target picture has a religious theme. Likewise, the correspondence could come as a *simile*, a *metaphor*, or even a *pun*. For each picture, you should explore in your mind any *possible association*, direct or indirect, that may exist between the picture and your impressions. These associations may be highly personal, but if they are real to you they may serve as important clues to the correct correspondence.

3. Your experience may not conform to the whole picture, but to a *part* of the picture. For example, the target may be a picture of a girl with long hair, and your impression might be, not of a girl, but of hair or something to do with hair.
4. Your impression may correctly reflect the *form*, but not the meaning of the picture. For example, a weather thermometer with a ball at one end might be incorrectly interpreted as a flagpole.
5. Finally, the picture may be represented in your experience not as an image, but as an *emotion or feeling*. For example, if you felt "closed in" during the test, the target might have something to do with a person or animal who is confined.

Direct or literal correspondences should generally be given higher ratings than indirect or symbolic correspondences, unless the latter are particularly meaningful or striking to you.

In rating the five pictures, do not compare one picture with another and rate on that basis—rather, rate each one *separately* on its own merits. You should make your rating of each picutre independent of your rating on any of the other pictures. Avoid the temptation to decide that a given picture *must* be the target, and therefore to arbitrarily give the other pictures low ratings. Do *not* ask yourself, "How much closer to my impressions is this picture than the others!" Instead, ask yourself only, "How well does this picture fit my impressions?"

ESP impressions also sometimes enter consciousness by way of memory traces. This is especially true when mental imagery is used to mediate the ESP impressions, since mental imagery is a function of memory. If the target were, for example, a picture of a whale, you might suddenly think about a whale you once saw at a marine exhibit. Just how or why this occurs is not known, though much research is underway in an attempt to find out. This process can be a very touchy one since it can confuse an inexperienced subject already trying to discriminate any possible ESP impressions he or she has received from the random wanderings of his own mind.

The best way to judge free response material is to carefully examine just how you tend to assimilate and generate ESP information. You will probably notice patterns in your responses that will help you identify ESP impressions more readily in the future.

_____appendix II:
ESP and drugs

Why is ESP such an enigma? The answer to this question has become clearer over the last few years. ESP is an unconscious process. First we receive ESP impressions unconsciously, and then those impressions have to fight their way into consciousness, so they mainly manifest in the form of hunches, visions, dreams, and even hallucinations. These are all modes the unconscious uses to push information into the conscious mind. A person is more likely to have an ESP experience when he is dreaming, daydreaming, or resting passively than when he is preoccupied with the frantic pace of day to day living in our high-pitched, supermechanized society. In other words, conscious ESP is a product of a state of mind and over the last thirty years investigators have isolated some of the mental states which seem particularly conducive to ESP. Hypnosis, dreaming, and sensory isolation all seem to place us in a mildly altered state of

This appendix contains the original text of an article which appeared in an edited version in the November 1977 issue of *High Times*. It seems wise to include this material since some people have deliberately used drugs to gain access to ESP powers. In no way should this report be construed as an endorsement of drug use. (This material is reprinted with the permission of *High Times*.)

awareness during which ESP impressions will surface into consciousness more readily. Why? Apparently, it is only when we shut out the outside world and its constant assault on our physical senses that we become aware of ESP messages. It is not hard to see why techniques for developing ESP place so much emphasis on meditation and quietude. In these states we are more attuned to our own thoughts and introspection.

Drugs have been used for this very purpose for centuries. Both primitive man and our modern drug culture enthusiasts have found that mind-altering drugs are (to borrow Freud's phrase) a royal road to the unconscious. Psychedelic drugs in particular envelop us in visions and emotions which burst forth from the unconscious. Could ESP be enhanced by hallucinogenic drugs? Some anecdotal reports and research findings suggest that it might, but the relationship is a controversial and uncertain one.

Even primitive man realized that mind-altering drugs could induce ESP experiences. In fact, the ritual ingestion of drugs to prompt ESP experiences was even recorded by the ancient Aztecs who ate psychogenic mushrooms in order to see visions of the future. These records are anything but folklore, for even contemporary explorers have reported dramatic cases of ESP powers which were exhibited by primitive peoples after ingesting psychedelic mushrooms, vines, and assorted brews.

Dr. William McGovern, who was assistant curator of South American ethnology at Field Museum of Natural History at the time, reported his own observations on primitive drug use in 1927. While exploring the little native settlements that dot the Amazon River, McGovern was able to witness a ritual which included the drinking of an hallucinogenic concoction processed from the *Banisteriopsis caapi* plant:

> ... [C]ertain of the Indians fell into a particularly deep state of trance in which they possessed what appeared to be telepathic powers. Two or three of the men described what was going on in *malokas* hundreds of miles away, many of which they had never visited, and the inhabitants of which they had never seen, but which seemed to tally exactly with what I knew of the places and people concerned. More extraordinary still, on this particular evening, the local medicine-man told me that the chief of a certain tribe in far away Pira Panama had suddenly died. I entered this statement in my diary and many weeks later, when we came to the tribe in question, I found that the witch-doctor's statements had been true in every detail ..."*

*Jungle Paths and Inca Ruins (New York: Grosset & Dunlap, 1927).

Dr. McGovern was not the only traveler to bring back such tales to the civilized world. Several other explorers have had similar experiences to report. So it wasn't long before European and American investigators began deliberately experimenting to see if any of the hallucinogens had telepathic properties.

The first experimental investigations into the question date back to the 1920s and '30s when French investigators got into the act at the Pasteur Institute in Paris. They gave mescaline to subjects and then tested to see how well they could reproduce sketches or words drawn and written in another room and sent to them telepathically. Apparently the experiments succeeded admirably because the Pasteur Institute researchers soon dubbed mescaline "the telepathic drug." At the same time private investigations were being carried out along similar lines by Dr. Eugene Osty, a well-known French parapsychologist of the day, on the effects of yagé on ESP.

Even Soviet scientists climbed aboard the bandwagon. Writing in his book, *Mysterious Phenomena of the Human Psyche*,* Leonid Vasiliev of the Institute for Brain Research in Leningrad admitted that he too had experimented in hopes of finding a relationship between mescaline and ESP. Vasiliev, who carried out his research in 1946, was probably the first contemporary parapsychologist to explore the ESP effects of psychedelic drugs.

Only one subject was used for his experiments. She was a physiologist who, according to the Soviet scientist "... gave no signs whatsoever of possessing parapsychological capabilities". The volunteer was given mescaline and two hours later, when she began describing intense mental imagery, Vasiliev asked her to psychically describe what objects were hidden in a series of black plastic boxes. Several of these trials were extremely successful. When the target was a postage stamp imprinted with a picture of the Central Telegraph Building in Moscow, the subject reported, "A stone house. How did you contrive to hide a house in there?" A bunch of red coral was described as, "something that is yellow, oval, hard, orange, and tinkles." A frog elicited the response, "... Something alive."

There can be little doubt that some of these impressions related directly to the objects in the boxes. Unfortunately, since Prof. Vasiliev did not test the subject before or after her mescaline experience, we really don't know how well she would have done on the ESP test in a normal

*New Hyde Park, N.Y.: University Books, 1965.

state of mind. Despite the fact that this pilot study was promising, Vasiliev never continued on with his drug research.

Now, you might ask, what about LSD?

LSD was synthesized in 1943 during a time when the study of ESP was still frowned upon in academic circles. Behaviorist psychology, which had neither interest nor respect for the subjective workings of the mind, was running rampant, so psychology was not overly interested in either LSD or ESP. The former experience was considered only a drug-induced model psychosis, while the latter was not even considered at all! But as investigators began studying the LSD experience, cases of spontaneous ESP started cropping up to their amazement.

Probably the two most active LSD investigators in this country have been the husband and wife team of R. E. L. Masters and Dr. Jean Houston. Although not originally interested in ESP, they were intrigued enough to study it experimentally when some of their subjects started reporting ESP impressions during their sessions. One incident occurred when a young housewife was given LSD during an experimental session monitored by the two investigators. As they record in their book, *The Varieties of Psychedelic Experience:**

> S-19 ... complained in the course of a LSD session that she could see her little girl in the kitchen of their home and that the daughter was taking advantage of her mother's absence to go looking for a cookie jar. S further reported that the daughter was standing on a chair and rummaging through the kitchen cabinets. She "saw" the child knock a glass sugar bowl from the shelf and remarked that the bowl had shattered on the floor, spilling sugar all around.

> S forgot about this episode, but when she returned home, after her session, she decided to make herself some coffee and then was unable to find the sugar bowl. She asked her husband where it was and he told her that while she was away their daughter had "made a mess" knocking the sugar bowl from the shelf and smashing it. The child had done this "while looking for cookies."

Another LSD-induced ESP experience was brought to Masters' and Houston's attention by a friend. He had been monitoring an LSD session when his subject reported seeing a ship caught in the ice in the northern seas. She even saw its name written on the bow, the *France*. Three days

---

*New York: Dell, 1966.

later, local newspapers reported that a ship, the *France*, had been freed from ice floes near Greenland.

Since ESP experiences do seem to happen all the time, there is no way of telling if the above incidents were specifically prompted by the LSD. Even though these two cases seem to be very well witnessed, they do not in themselves offer very strong evidence for an LSD-ESP relationship. So Masters and Houston began to experimentally explore the relationship to see if one really did exist.

For their first project, Masters and Houston tested 27 LSD subjects with standard ESP (Zener) cards. These are the well-known cards which J. B. Rhine developed and made famous at Duke University. The deck consists of a sequence of 25 cards, each of which is printed with one of five geometric symbols; either a cross, star, circle, square, or wavy lines. By calling the sequence of twenty-five cards, the subject might be expected to get about 5 correct by chance. Jean Houston acted as agent and, sitting across the room from the subject, concentrated on the cards one by one, attempting to psychically influence the subject's guesses. Twenty-three of the subjects scored at chance. However 4 of the subjects did seem to score above average, and only one of them continued to score well when tested later after the effects of the drug had worn off.

Masters and Houston soon discovered, though, that their subjects quickly wearied of guessing cards and became bored with the whole thing. So they changed strategy. For a new series of tests they prepared slips of paper with images described on them. The agent, again sitting across the room from the subject, picked up the slips one by one and tried to telepathically send the image to the intoxicated subject. Better results seemed to be obtained with this more interesting method.

Sometimes the subjects were extremely accurate when they described what they thought was being mentally transmitted to them. When a target was a Viking ship tossing in a storm, one subject reported, "Snake with arched head swimming in tossed seas". When the target was a tropical rain forest, the same subject reported imaging, "Lush vegetation, exotic flowers, startling green—all seen through watery mist."

Masters and Houston approximated that out of the 63 subjects that they tested, at least 48 of them achieved some success on at least one or two of the imagery attempts while five had more consistent success.

By no means, though, have all parapsychologists had the same level of success as Masters and Houston reported. In fact, most LSD-ESP tests have been total washouts.

One of the most systematic investigations into the effects of psychedelic drugs on ESP was a lengthy project carried out by two Italian investigators, Roberto Cavanna and Emilio Servadio. The team was an ideal one. Cavanna is a prominent pharmacologist, while Servadio is one of Italy's leading parapsychologists. For their project, the two investigators utilized LSD and psilocybin.

Subjects for the tests were first selected during initial interviewing, and then were invited to return to the experimental premises. They were asked to sit in a comfortable room where they were given mild doses of either of the hallucinogens. After the drug had taken effect, they were asked to describe pictures sealed in closed envelopes. These pictures were surrealistic, especially designed to appeal to the unworldliness of the psychedelic experience. Among the target pictures was a baby doll's head in a glass, a hand with a tiny hand emerging from between two of its fingers, a key held in clenched teeth, a foot balancing a glass eye, and so on.

Despite the care in which the experiments were run, Cavanna and Servadio soon discovered that only rarely did their subjects ever get any impressions which seemed linked to the target. It seemed as though ESP didn't even exist. Sometimes though, but very rarely, there were vague hits. One subject guessed "gargoyles" when the target was a picture of a rather caricature-like doll. The best response of the whole project came from one man who had been given LSD. The target was the picture of the hands described above. He reported, "... from a black thing the finger points of the huge hand come out ..."

These "hits" were very scattered and it is not difficult to believe that coincidence could account for them. So Cavanna and Servadio gave up their project but did write a monograph, *ESP Experiments with LSD 25 and Psilocybin*, which was published by the Parapsychology Foundation in 1964.

Cavanna and Servadio were not the only ones to fail in their search for a drug-ESP relationship. Three Dutch experimenters—S. van Asperen deBoer, P. Barkenna, and Jan Kappers—tested hallucinating subjects with standard ESP cards and for psychometry. (Psychometry is the ability to gain psychic impressions from handling physical objects.) They came up with a flat zero.*

LSD-ESP experiments were also conducted by Dr. Walter Pahnke at the Maryland Psychiatric Research Center in Baltimore. For his tests, an

*International Journal of Neuropsychiatry, 1966, 26, 431-61.

experimenter was seated in one room of the center in front of a box with five windows, each of which was printed with one of the five ESP card symbols. When the box was activated, one of the windows would illuminate thereby designating a target. The subject was placed in another room and sat before a duplicate box and had to guess which symbol was being viewed by the agent. Five subjects were first tested in a normal state and then under the influence of LSD.

Pahnke, sad to say, achieved only very poor results. Reporting on his experiments to the 1970 Conference of the Parapsychology Foundation in Le Piol, France, he had to conclude:

> Preliminary findings on these five subjects in our pilot study have not demonstrated that LSD can enhance psi performance under these conditions. In no case was there a significant increase of the LSD performance over the pre-drug performance. In one case, however, there was a marked decrease in scoring ability ...

Pahnke was not totally pessimistic, though. In his report he suggested that the setting of the test, dosage, and the relationship between the experimenter and the subject could have significant bearing on the LSD-ESP relationship and could have caused the failure of his design. Pahnke also suggested that drugs other than LSD might be more suited to ESP testing and singled out STP and MDA as likely candidates.* But he was forced to conclude nevertheless:

> Throughout the history of parapsychological research there have been hints and suggestions that certain drugs might modify the results of psi performance. Some have been anecdotal experiences, and others have been when drugs were given during parapsychological experiments. Up to the present, no clear-cut or substantial effect of any drug has been demonstrated ...

Dr. Pahnke had hoped to continue his research, but his untimely death during a diving trip put an end to his work.

So there you have it. There is an obvious contradiction here between the work reported by the Pasteur Institute and Masters and Houston and

*STP is the street name for DOM, an intense long-lasting psychedelic somewhat similar to LSD. MDA is a methoxylated amphetamine which is also psychedelic and which acts to enhance mood and thinking without (usually) becoming hallucinogenic.

the negligible results of Pahnke, Cavanna and Servadio among others. Why? Is there an LSD-ESP relationship or isn't there?

One reason why we have such conflicting reports on the LSD-ESP relationship might be because some of the experimenters ran their tests in such a way as to ensure failure. There researchers might have taken a clue from more mainline LSD research. When psychedelic drug research first became prominent, psychologists quickly learned that it was very hard for drug intoxicated subjects to settle down and fill out a questionnaire or take psychological tests. The trippers simply didn't want to be distracted from their experience, from their subjective sensations, or from their introspective journeys. Not only did they have a difficult time focusing on psychological tests, but many subjects made it quite clear they didn't even *want* to cooperate!

A similar problem might have cropped up in some of these LSD-ESP tests. The subjects probably just didn't want to be bothered. Masters and Houston found that their subjects grew bored very quickly with card-guessing tests and even Pahnke realized that his highly structured experiment might have defeated its own purpose.

I think I can make this whole problem a little clearer by describing a pilot ESP experiment of my own during which we ran into the same difficulty. I was testing subjects for ESP in a Lilly-type isolation tank. The subject had to describe over a speaking unit all of his mental images as he floated in the tank. We tried to telepathically affect what he was describing by concentrating on a reel of viewmaster pictures. I soon gave up the experiment. It became painfully clear that the subjects were so enthralled by the novel physical sensations prompted by the tank that they didn't want to be distracted from it by talking to me over the intercom. It was too distracting to talk, and my subjects soon lost all interest in the ESP test. Under this condition, it was hardly likely that we would get any results. For good ESP performance, subjects have to be enthusiastic and motivated. These same factors could easily have occurred during some of the less successful ESP-LSD experiments. They also explain why ESP might occur spontaneously in a free, unstructured ESP test, but not when ESP is being rigidly and systematically tested for.

Because of the tight legal regulations on even scientific LSD research, the search for a relationship between psychic ability and the hallucinogens stopped prematurely a decade ago. Now, however, parapsychologists are focusing a not-too-disinterested eye on LSD-induced psychic effects thanks to some startling discoveries recently announced by one of this country's leading LSD authories, Dr. Stanislov Grof. Dr. Grof's work is bound to reopen the entire issue.

Dr. Grof has been involved in investigating several different aspects of LSD over the years. He began his research in Czechoslovakia in 1956 and from 1967–73 he continued his explorations at the Maryland Psychiatric Research Center where Dr. Pahnke also worked. He is now associated with the Esalen Institute in Big Sur, California.

Dr. Grof's book, *Realms of the Human Unconscious—observations from LSD research,** is bound to create quite a stir among both his professional colleagues and the parapsychological community. He has no qualms about admitting that he has observed remarkable ESP demonstrations by his subjects. In fact, he admits that he has witnessed an entire hierarchy of ESP effects. He has stated, for example, that his subjects sometimes begin to identify with their own ancestors and "... convey specific information that was unknown to the subject, and, in some instances, not even accessible to him at the time of the session."

Other subjects, claims Grof, identify with animals and seem to gain an unexplained and apparently extrasensory understanding and knowledge of their physiology and behavior.

One of Dr. Grof's most spectacular cases concerns a 50-year-old psychologist named Nadja who was undergoing a LSD training session. During her experience she relived a series of events in the life of her mother and she mentally reenacted a scene in which "she" was hiding under a staircase in fear when suddenly someone put a hand over her mouth. Asking her mother about the incident, the elder woman verified the accuracy of the scene as her daughter had relived it.

Was this ESP or perhaps even genetic memory? (Of course, genetic memory is an issue easily as controversial as ESP.)

Dr. Grof worked more intensively with another subject named Renata who, during LSD therapy, began reliving scenes from 17th century Czechoslovakia. She described people, scenes, historical facts, architecture, etc. of the period although she had never studied this particular epoch of Czech history. Grof himself spent hours trying to verify the impressions and facts related to him by his patient and gradually was able to corroborate a vast number of them. He also reports, as mentioned above, that LSD subjects often seem to create a psychic bond with animal life:

*New York: Viking, 1975.

"It is not uncommon," Grof writes, "for subjects reporting evolutionary experiences to manifest a detailed knowledge of the animals with whom they have identified—of their physical characteristics, habits, and behavior patterns—that far exceeds their educations in the natural sciences. On occasion subjects have accurately described courtship dances, complicated reproductive cycles, techniques of nest-building, patterns of aggression and defense, and many zoological and ethological facts about the animals they have experienced in sessions."

Dr. Grof admits, all in all, that the experimental research on the LSD-ESP question has been mixed. Nevertheless, in light of the results of his own work, he offers no apologies when he concludes in his book that, "... states conducive to various paranormal phenomena and characterized by unusually high incidence of ESP are, however, among the many alternative conditions that can be facilitiated by the drug."

The reason for Grof's success may lay in the fact that, unlike Pahnke and Cavanna and Servadio, he has never tried to force ESP out into the open. Instead he has allowed it to manifest by itself in the course of his therapeutic work. This free and non-demand setting might be a perfect one for ESP to manifest.

With the work of Dr. Grof looming before us, perhaps parapsychologists will once again take a serious look at the psychedelic drugs to see if they can be of aid as we search to understand ESP. At the very least it is obvious that more research is needed on the question.

Even if a relationship between ESP and LSD, or any drug for that matter, is found, what will it tell us about the ESP process? As I stated at the opening of this report, ESP is an unconscious process, and our main problem is coaxing it out into the open. Drugs will never be the total solution to this problem, only a temporary catalyst. It is not the drug which helps manifest the ESP, but the state of mind the drug produces. If ESP is a product of a specific state of mind, as many younger parapsychologists believe, then LSD will not be a means in itself. It will only be a temporary tool.

Index

172

CPSIA information can be obtained
at www.ICGtesting.com
Printed in the USA
BVHW032012050920
588149BV00001B/18